Aligned & Engaged

Hidden Keys for Turning Teamwork into Profit

By Kevin F. Fox

For information about permission to reproduce selections from this book or to inquire about special discounts for bulk purchases, please email:

kfox@myviablevision.com

A catalog record of this book is available from the Library of Congress

ISBN# 978-0-692-54350-4

www.teamworkforprofit.com

For Robert, Ryan, and Emmett

I look forward to reading your books one day

Table of Contents

Acknowledgments

Chapter 1: Teamwork and Profits.. 1

Chapter 2: Connecting Team Work to Profits 11

Chapter 3: Building a Profitable Team...19

Chapter 4: Practices for Alignment 25

Practice 1: *Communicate the Goal* 29

Practice 2: *Share Bottom Line Results with Everyone* 32

Practice 3: *Replace Local Measures with Global Ones* 34

Practice 4: *Find the Constraint of your Business* 36

Practice 5: *Blue Light your Business* 40

Practice 6: *Use T,I, and OE to Align Decisions with the Goal* 44

Practice 7: *Routinely Review and Re-Align Your Measures* 47

Practice 8: *Map what Good Alignment Looks Like*............................51

Practice 9: *Spend Most of your Time and Energy on Today* 55

Practice 10: *Pareto to Stop Wasting Effort* 57

Practice 11: *Stop the Multi-Tasking* 60

Practice 12: *Relate Everything Back to the Big Picture* 65

Practice 13: *Focus on Throughput* 68

Practice 14: *Use Measures to Provide Fast Feedback on Ideas* 71

Chapter 5: Practices for Engagement.. 75

Practice 15: *Picture What Engagement Looks Like* 79

Practice 16: *Innovate on Process* 81

Practice 17: *Communicate 'What Good Looks Like'* 84

Practice 18: *Spark Creative Problem Solving* 88

Practice 19: *Catch People Doing Something Right*............................92

Practice 20: *Share Your Ideas Last* 95

Practice 21: *Provide Opportunities for Growth* 97

Practice 22: *Use Questions* 100

Practice 23: *Stop the B-Game* 103

Practice 24: *Rebuild Trust with Appreciations* 106

Practice 25: *Get Out and Walk Around Everyday* 108

Practice 26: *Follow Through Quickly* 110

Practice 27: *Become the Obstacle Breaker* 112

Practice 28: *Use Financial Incentives Very Carefully* 114

Practice 29: *Expect the Best from People* 116

Chapter 6: An On-going Practice...119

Afterword..126

Practice Reference Tables 128

End Notes 130

About the Author 133

Acknowledgments

This book is a product of my 30 years of professional life and it bears the imprint of hundreds of people I have had the pleasure and privilege to work with and learn from. I am grateful to my parents, Bob and Loretta Fox, who started me on my journey and who have supported me in immeasurable ways at every step. My father was wise and unfailing as my main professional mentor, later as a business partner, and as a central editor of this book. My mother's support and encouragement gave me confidence to grow and learn. I owe them a debt of gratitude I can never repay.

So many of my colleagues, clients, and friends contributed to the knowledge in this book. Virtually everything here was gleaned, shaped or created from the work and expertise of those people. I was blessed by my long association with Dr. Eli Goldratt and his insights and the spirit of his work is all over this book. My remarkable colleagues in consulting, Ravi Gilani, Henry Camp, Bart Penrod, Mark Woeppel, Ron Wilder, Mike Hannan and my longtime partner Ken Pasterczyk provided their wisdom and helped to shape and strengthen so many of the practices contained here. Professors James Cox and James Holt, long supporters of mine were great role models for me in shaping my ideas for the book. Authors John Covington, Bob Sproull and Bruce Nelson, whose writings helped inspire me to start this work, provided invaluable feedback on the text. My friend and colleague, Sanjeev Gupta, in his characteristic style, read and commented on my draft in less than 24 hours, giving me several nuggets of pure gold. My brother Brendan, whose deep thinking always forced me to see things I thought I understood in new ways, was force in the back of my mind throughout my writing.

My friends in government service—Alfredo Mycue, Kristen Cox, Greg Gardner, Steve Cuthbert, Rick Little, Larry Temple, and Jon Pierpont—challenged me in so many ways helping along the way to make so many of these practices more tangible and easy to apply. Friends Ron Stephens, Randy Christensen and Tim Schultz were supportive and gave freely of their time to review my drafts.

Lastly, I owe a great debt of gratitude to my brother Michael, and my wife and professional editor, Amy. Michael spent hours discussing my ideas for the book and helping to shape its form, and structure, on top of the years of encouragement and kind guidance he has given me. Amy was the force who helped me push this over the edge, from an idea to a reality. She has probably read the book more times than I have and her expertise and strength as an editor are only exceeded by her ability to encourage and support me and this work. Thank you. And thank you all.

Aligned & Engaged

Chapter 1

Teamwork and Profits

"Individual commitment to a group effort – that's what makes a team work, a company work, a society work, a civilization work."
                                                                        -Vince Lombardi

Teamwork (n.) –work done by several associates with each doing a part but all subordinating personal prominence to the efficiency of the whole[1]

Business has always valued the importance of teamwork, and it's only becoming more important to success. Technology is giving customers and investors choice on a global scale, creating performance expectations that are growing all the time. Additionally, the growing complexity and inter-connectedness of our companies and supply chains is naturally placing a premium on how the ability to manage these "teams". Whether it is being faster, more nimble, efficient, or reliable, more flexible, adaptable or responsive, leaders must find ways to create better and better teamwork.

Improving teamwork is no longer a checklist item of the HR department, it is an essential skill and daily responsibility of leaders at all levels. It's not a skill that most have been well prepared in though. Team building has traditionally not been viewed as a first-tier management skill like planning, strategy, functional expertise or financial literacy. So for most leaders a deeper understanding of the essential elements of teamwork and how to develop them are vital and valuable capabilities to possess.

And it starts with a 'simple' and basic question every leader needs to ask: *"What is my job in leading my team?"*

There are many possible answers and I suggest you take a moment to formulate your own. In my experience there are a host of successful strategies, techniques and approaches to leading successful teams— whether it is in business, the non-profit world, sports or anything else. You can probably think of almost as many different styles as the number of successful leaders and teams you can bring to mind. In my mind there is only one true answer to the question.

Some will think of the more philosophical areas and say the job of a leader is to provide a compelling vision or to inspire and motivate the team. Establishing a great culture of success might fit in here as well. Others may think of it in the managerial sense; conceiving of the job as one of listening, developing, and guiding people to perform at their best. Another way of looking at it is to see it from a process standpoint, establishing the right measures, roles, and guidelines for the organization. There is the skill perspective, pointing to assembly of the right team members with the right knowledge and skills to excel. Of course there is the strategic point of view, where we might see the job as making great decisions, and providing a sharp focus for the company.

I am sure I have missed at least a few of the many other common answers to the question. While each of these is valid, none of them ultimately is the job of the leader of the team. The job of the leader is very simple—it is to help the team 'win.'

In sports, great teams win games and championships. They achieve their goals. Great business teams achieve their goals as well or we simply do not call them successful. For the vast majority of businesses that goal is to make more money now and in the future. The role of the leader is to do whatever it takes to ensure the company reaches that goal--nothing more and nothing less. All of the rest of it, the vision, the right people, the roles and responsibilities and the strategy are all *means* to achieve the end of helping the company win.

Why does this matter? It matters because how you see your job determines what you will do and how you will act. If you see your job is to set the focus of the company, then that is what you will do. In other words, you will limit the role you play to your view of the job. When we put such limits on ourselves and our role, we are less likely to consider other actions or roles we might need to play to make the company successful. It's critical to have a broad and expansive view of our role in order to create a winning team.

The Flaws of Teamwork Initiatives

Every manager if asked will tell you teamwork is vital to success. Many of these same managers will also tell you teamwork initiatives make them uneasy. This paradox stems from the flawed way many pursue improving teamwork in companies. Teamwork is all-too-often undertaken as something "apart" from the business.

We are encouraged to do "team-building activities," often off-site or away from the business itself, as if it were some kind of extra-curricular activity. As Allan Cox, author of a dozen books on business management and advisor to CEO's and corporate boards, puts it, "Team-building has been practiced in most cases as a special activity and carried out by second- and third-level human resources professionals or consultants."[2]

Having a 'bonding experience' can be nice, and people generally do leave them feeling positive, but these activities do little (or nothing) to change the fundamental realities *within* the company. Moreover, the teams we work with every day are not led or managed by HR staff or external consultants; they only intervene a couple of times a year. They are run by the managers responsible every day for that part of the business. So unless the changes come from them, it's hard to imagine much will change.

Another frequent way teamwork is introduced is through activities to strengthen the component skills effective teams' usually possess, like communication, empathy, listening, and cooperation. Of course these skills are valuable. But the assumption here is that poor teamwork is essentially a behavioral or 'people' problem. Think for a moment when teamwork issues and conflict became apparent in your business. If the issues didn't appear suddenly but grew up gradually over time, and are present between people who have worked together for some time, it's not likely a people problem, it's a system problem.

In all likelihood, issues or situations **within the business** put people at odds with each other. They didn't have trouble cooperating the day they met, the difficulty arose out of the business. The problem is deeper than poor communication or mis-understanding between people—those are just the symptoms. Treating the symptoms may dampen or mask them for a time, but it does not remove the underlying cause. Something within your company is misaligned, producing the symptoms you observe. It might be local objectives putting people into conflict, unclear roles, or something else, but the problem is systemic and if you don't address, it's not going away, no matter how many workshops you do, or how many new people you inject into the company.

As social scientist, TEDx speaker, and co-founder of Creating the Future, Hildy Gottlieb reports, "We have yet to find a situation where the perceived need for Team Building doesn't somehow stem from problems at the root of the organization."[3]

I understand completely why so many managers get uneasy when the subject of improving teamwork comes up. If their experience is anything like this, they already know it will likely be a waste of time and money. Teamwork is something that must be built within the organization, by the managers, and in the daily reality of the business. Falling backward into your co-workers arms may build trust they will catch you, but it doesn't teach us anything about running a successful company.

There are two lessons from such failed approaches. First, if you want teamwork to be what it should be, a driver of profit and growth for your business, it cannot be something that is done outside of the context of your business. Second, it cannot address only the apparent symptoms, it must work at the level of the underlying causes, or it is doomed to failure. Paraphrasing Allan Cox from many years ago, "teamwork must do real work, and it must be corporate wide."[4] Teamwork is not so much something the business does, like marketing or product development, as it is *how* you do everything. If you want real results for your business it's vital to keep teamwork firmly within the context and operation of your business, and ingrain that in the minds of your managers and team.

Teamwork in Your Business Context

I have played and been around sports virtually all of my life, and I have never once heard a coach say we're going to stop practice and work on teamwork now. Once your company strategy is in place, all the rest of the work of the business, the execution, is about teamwork. In sports, teamwork was always about achieving the goal of the team— scoring the goal, defending your own, and winning the game. It is no different for your business. Teamwork is the means to achieving the company's goal.

Put simply, business teamwork is about 'getting people to work together in a way that helps the company grow, profit, and beat the competition.' Serving the customers, offering great value, and providing a rewarding work environment are important means to that goal, but they are not the goal. Making more and more money is the goal of virtually all "for-profit" companies. This is a good thing, too, because making money is very tangible and easily measured. It provides an objective way to evaluate performance, as well as the decisions we make and the actions we take. It also enables us to define what good teamwork is and isn't. Efforts that move us toward the goal are good for the team, those that don't are not.

To be sure, there are many factors which contribute to overall business success. You must have a great value proposition, an excellent product or service, an adequate market, ample technical skills, and many other things. Teamwork is not the only factor in success, but it is an important one. A football team with great teamwork may still lose the game to another team if they are not fast enough or big enough. Better teamwork will always improve your results.

Teamwork helps you increase efficiency and effectiveness, serve your customers better, create better products, and improve just about every facet of your company that impacts your success. By working on teamwork you can expect two important things to happen:

1. You will get better and better results out of your business

2. Any gaps in your business or organization will become more evident, enabling you to better address them

This book is about putting teamwork back in its original and proper place, at the heart of what you do and how you do it. Teamwork must be woven into your routine business operations to execute your strategy and reach your goals. It isn't something that's nice to have, or something we pay attention to when we have the luxury to do so. It's how you produce results in the company.

Your company is already functioning as a team, you wouldn't be in business otherwise. To take your company and yourself to the next level you need to improve that teamwork. Remember the job of leading the team is "to help the team to win."

What Really Matters for Business Teams

To build a highly successful business team, it helps to understand the two critical components or aspects of great teamwork:

Alignment and *Engagement*

Alignment relates to how people work together or in collaboration with each other, toward the common goal. Engagement is the level commitment, effort and 'striving' individuals put forth on behalf of the team. Too often, this distinction is overlooked or muddled, making it difficult to determine what each business needs to improve performance. Both elements are important, and achieving each requires a different approach and a different set of actions. Learning the distinction between them will enable you to better assess your business needs and increase your ability to take effective action.

Alignment

Every successful business team must be aligned in two ways. The team must be aligned with the goal of the business, and they must be aligned with each other in how they pursue that goal. Being aligned with the goal doesn't mean every employee must care as much as the owners do about growing profits, but it means their efforts, actions, and decisions must be focused narrowly on that end.

The team should also be aligned with each other in how it is pursues the goal. A football team's aim may be to score a touchdown, but it does not mean all the players grab for the ball and try to run to the end zone. To reach the common goal, each plays a role coordinated and aligned with the others, enabling the team move the ball down the field toward its goal. When a company is not aligned well, there are a host of apparent symptoms, including 'silos,' where one part of the organization seems at odds with the others. Diagnosing these symptoms will be discussed in the next chapter.

Engagement

Engagement is the act of getting the best out of your people, coaching them to do great work in fulfilling their roles. As with any team not every role or person is equal, nor will they ever. The tight end on the football team is important, but rarely will his role be as important to the team's success as the quarterback's. Wise leaders know to focus on critical roles, recognizing engaging some individuals will add disproportionately more to the company. Engagement is infectious, when a few people go the extra mile, it catches on quickly.

Expanding the success of your business team is a process of continually improving the alignment and engagement of your team. They are already aligned and engaged to a certain degree, and the better they work effectively together the more engaged they become; the better your performance will be.

An effective business leader is continually seeking to identify where better alignment or engagement will contribute most to results. Depending on your current situation, the bigger opportunity will lie in one or the other area. Neither is inherently more important than the other, though understanding which component is most lacking will help you accelerate results.

What Makes this Book Different?

Creating an effective team producing higher and higher profits has three important aspects:

- Focus on your goal (making more and more money if you are a for-profit business)

- Alignment with the goal and across the organization
- Engagement to bring out people's best

This book is about providing you tools and tangible steps you can take to achieve these essential elements in your business. Many of these are things you already know. I call them "practices," because ultimately they are activities performed regularly to strengthen your team. Good business leaders know very well, success is almost never the result of some "silver bullet." It comes from habit, from consistent and repeated effort.

Most of the practices here are rightly called common sense. It should come as no surprise most companies are already doing these or similar things, and have already built many of the qualities of successful teams. However, common sense is not always common practice. There is often a gap between what we know and what we do. Having structured, easy-to-follow practices helps us to close this gap. It's always easier to lean on a process than it is to think our way through an issue or to invent our own solutions every time. As humans we are creatures of habit, and these practices will reinforce the effective practices you need to create a more successful and profitable business.

If you look at the best teams in any field of pursuit you will find they do all three of these things very well, even if they do not fully understand it. Great teams are always focused on their goal. The various parts work seamlessly as one, each playing its role effectively in concert with the others. And the people on great teams perform at a very high level. They do their best work, go the extra mile, and find ways to get it done. They understand that their only real job is to "help the company win."

Chapter 2

Connecting Teamwork

to Profits

"Coming together is a beginning. Keeping together is progress. Working together is success."   *-Henry Ford*

We know at a gut-level teamwork is important to success. But the connection between individual actions and the financial performance of the company is murky. Whenever there is a choice between doing something clearly aligned with the goal of the company, and something vague and uncertain, the clear choice will win out every time. I think this explains why most companies take such an ambivalent stance on team work and team building. We become even more ambivalent when teamwork requires time or money from us. This is why companies are much more likely to invest in building better teams in good times than in more difficult ones.

As with any activity or investment we make in our business, the value is in the return we get from it. We want to put our efforts and money toward things that will create tangible paybacks for our company. In other words it's about our Return-on Investment (ROI). With teamwork, ROI is often hard to determine or it requires a long time to realize the results. However, there are several ways to strengthen the connection, and improve the magnitude and certainty of your ROI from your team-building efforts.

One way to improve ROI is to reduce the net investment required to do the activity. To this end none of the activities in this book require any financial investment, that is, beyond what you paid to purchase this book. They do require some investment of your most precious resource though, your time. With this in mind I have carefully selected and designed the practices in the book to require minimal time to implement. And to ensure teamwork is always firmly in the idle of your business context, none of the activities are done apart from or separate from the regular work of the business. They are modifications or enhancements to things you are already doing. In most cases they will actually free-up or create more time for you and your organization as a whole. So the net investment will actually be a positive and not a negative. You will end up with more time and not less.

The real benefit of better teamwork is better business performance— more profits, more growth, or however you define it in your company. Many years ago Eli Goldratt suggested three common sense measures in his landmark business novel **The Goal.**[1] I like them because they are highly intuitive, easy for someone who isn't a CPA to understand, and they connect nicely to how most companies measure their overall financial performance.

> **Throughput (T)** The rate of generating revenues—which we want more of
>
> **Operating Expense (OE)** The money we spend to run our business—which we want to reduce

Investment (I) The money we have tied up in things like inventory, buildings and equipment—which we also want to reduce

These common sense measures bring the complexity of financial accounting to a level where everyone can understand how actions impact the goal of making money. In order for the company to make more money an action or decision needs to:

- Increase the money we generate—Throughput

- Reduce the money we spend to run the business—Operating Expense

- Reduce the money we have tied up and cannot use— Investment

Decisions or actions moving <u>all the measures</u> in the right direction help the company to make more money. If an action will move a measure in the wrong direction—let's say it will increase OE—it may still be a good idea. But it must be one of the other measures—T or I in this case— even more in the right direction. So for instance, hiring an additional Engineer will increase spending, OE. If that Engineer will enable us to increase T by three times his salary by enabling us to ship more, it's surely a good decision for the company.

It is also easy to connect Goldratt's three measurements to common bottom line measures, like Net Profit and Return on Investment, most companies already use in their financial statements. Net Profit, in common sense terms, is simply all the money we have left over from what we have generated, after we have paid all of our expenses. Return on Investment (ROI), is simply the "return" or Net Profit we have gotten, divided by the money invested in the company. The following diagram shows the formulas.

Net Profit = T - OE

Return on Investment = T – OE / I

Connecting teamwork activities to the goal of making money through these common sense measurements is no different from any other action. The work you do to improve teamwork should produce a net positive impact on Throughput, Investment, and Operating Expense. Remember, our job is to help the company win, which for the majority of companies means to make more money. The value of teamwork is to help us get to that goal, so keeping the measures in mind is a helpful way to stay on track.

Still, connecting teamwork efforts to financial measures is a bit of a new concept to most so it can be challenging. To make it easier to link your efforts to generating profits, I've created the **Profit Booster** labels which categorize how each of the teamwork practices in the work helps you increase profits.

Profit Boosters

Profit Boosters are a quick, easy and intuitive way to connect teamwork efforts to performance. Each of the practices in the book is labeled with the Profit Booster(s) it helps you improve. As you implement one of the practices you can monitor your results through the Profit Boosters. Additionally you can use the Profit Booster labels to select practices based on the type of improvement you are seeking. The four Profit Boosters are:

1. Creating Time ○
2. Doing the Right Things ◎
3. Doing Things Right 👍
4. Magnifying Impact ➕

Each of the practices in this book is labeled with the symbols above according to which one or two profit boosters it most impacts. A table at the end of the book shows all the practices and the profit booster connections. The profit booster labels help select practices to drive the type of improvement you want. If you have too much on your plate, choosing a couple of *Creating Time* ⏱ practices will help you free up the time you need to focus on bigger things. Maybe you are observing that your team is unfocused or tackling too many things at once. Finding some practices you like with the *Doing the Right Things* 🎯 label will help you get them back on track. Here's a more detailed description of how each of the profit booster labels can help you get the most from your efforts.

Creating Time ⏱

Management attention is probably the biggest constraint in any business. We only have so many things we can devote our attention to. Anything freeing up our time enables us to devote more attention elsewhere to grow profits. One of the chief considerations is the practice should not require a large commitment of time to implement. In addition, many of the practices are great for creating time. This happens in couple of ways.

A practice might replace something you are already doing which is requiring too much of your time. It also could prevent certain things from happening over time that drain resources from you and your team. In other instances, the practice will transfer work you are doing to another person(s) or level of the organization where the work can be done very effectively without your constant involvement. These practices to free up your time are often a great place to start, because until you can find a little time, it's difficult to focus on other things.

Doing the Right Things 🎯

Not everything is equally important, we all know that. Some things will, by their nature, give us greater returns than others. So choosing what we work on and what our teams work on is vital to the success of the business. Work on the activities with the greatest returns, and your business will grow faster and be more profitable. Work on things with small returns, or no returns, and that is what you will get.

A number of the practices in the book are designed to improve the ability of your organization to work on the right things. Accomplishing this is not a trivial task, because there are far more things that could be done, than we have the time or resources to do. Great teams don't often do everything well, but they always do the most important things well. A number of the techniques, particularly in the Alignment chapter, are expressly designed to help your team do more of the right things. If your team is struggling to focus properly, or is working hard but not having the desired impact, the practices with the bulls-eye symbol are a great place for you to start.

Doing Things Right 👍

Choosing the right things to do is important, and so is doing those things right or well. Great teams execute the work exceptionally well. When you do a great job on something you serve your customers better, improve quality, incur lower costs, and create fewer problems to solve later. Doing things right translates directly into more Throughput, less Expense, and lower Investment. Most of the 'Doing Things Right,' practices are located in Chapter 5 on Engagement. If you need to drive more of your team's actions to perform effectively and efficiently look for the thumbs-up symbol.

Magnifying Impact ⊕

Leverage is a key principle in any business. The greater the leverage, the greater the returns you will get. Successful teams don't just rely on their stars, they raise the level of all the players.

Magnifying impact practices are all about expanding your reach— making poor performers into good performers, and good ones great. This is accomplished when you transfer more and more correct decision making and responsibility downward in the organization. When the front line person knows how to effectively handle more situations, you get better results and have fewer problems to correct later.

Magnifying Impact practices multiply your effectiveness and drive profits much faster than before. Imagine having fifty or one hundred people taking the correct actions most of the time, versus relying only on your best people.

Keeping the Goal at the Center of Teamwork

Teamwork and your company's goal of making more and more money are interwoven. The goal is the purpose of your team and it is the guide for evaluating every action or decision. Understanding how your actions and decisions create profits is critical in every business. Using T, I, OE yourself and with your team to determine the impact of your actions will improve your results immensely. Being mindful of this connection and evaluating your performance is the only real way to ensure that teamwork will pay off for you.

Wherever you find the profit connection is not so clear or easy to establish, the Profit Boosters will help you determine which actions are leading you forward and which are not. A company that always has its goal front and center, and has more and more effective ways to measure its actions, will find itself on a steep upward performance curve. Sometimes the profit outcomes will not be immediate, as is the case with improving your diet or embarking on an exercise program. The Profit Boosters give you an intermediate signal to evaluate progress and stay on course.

Teamwork and business profits go hand in hand. The connection is not always as simple as some other aspects of running a business. Keep your goal top of mind, and link your efforts to your bottom line. You will see your efforts pay off.

Chapter 3

Building a Profitable Team

"Champions are made, not born." –The Book of Samuel.

Great athletic teams win, and great businesses grow their profits year after year. To achieve such success your team needs to have two critical qualities: Alignment and Engagement.

Alignment means everyone is pulling together, working in a highly coordinated way to achieve the goal. Engagement is the process of bringing out the best in your team members, getting them to perform at higher and higher levels as they work toward the goal. Increasing engagement and alignment will produce better and better profits, and strengthen the company for the future.

There are many examples of companies using alignment and engagement to foster the kind of teamwork to produce great result.

GE, during the time Jack Welch was CEO, was famous for creating very high levels of engagement among its staff and getting people aligned to the goal of making money. Apple is another example of these two traits at work. Their team alignment enabled them to deliver a steady stream of innovative products, and the engagement of their staff (as well as their customers) is direct evidence of the kind of commitment and energy great teams exhibit.

A great team of many people performing at their best and acting as one to deliver a great product or service, produce a beautiful symphony, truly something to marvel at and appreciate. You have probably had at least a few experiences like this, even if they temporary, in your own career. There is something deep and fundamental about us as people that makes us want to be part of a great, successful, winning team. As effortless as such high-functioning teams often appear from the outside, creating them is not a trivial thing to do.

The first step in the process is to understand the two critical dimensions of great teams so you can create the right mix of alignment and engagement to move your team forward. Most managers can sense whether they need to get more out of their people (engagement) or to get them to work more effectively together (alignment). Be sensitive to the symptoms of misalignment and lack of engagement. You will be in a better position to target the right improvements to take your team to the next level.

Recognizing Misalignment

Organizations with poor alignment work at cross-purposes with each other, rather than in synchronization. Misalignment happens all of the time in companies and battling it is an ongoing activity. It has some distinct symptoms or signs for recognition.

- *Silos* Whenever there are barriers or misalignment between parts of the organization, we recognize this as silos. Silos exist when following the objectives of one department lead to clashes with another. You will see people at odds with each other, complaining about what someone else did, mistrust, or finger-pointing, etc.

- *Problems appear late in the game* If you find problems are showing up late in your delivery process, or even at the customer, it's a strong indicator of misalignment. It means someone didn't understand the expectations, have all the right information, or put a departmental target over doing the job right to begin with. When a business is well-aligned, problems surface earlier, at the source and don't get passed on very often.

- *Department measures look good, but company performance doesn't* It's not possible for every department to be performing "well" and the company to not be performing well. Whenever this is the case, the most likely culprit is misalignment. In this case the indicators and incentives for the department are probably out of line with what is truly best for the company.

- *Local Improvements don't show up on the bottom line* Done properly improvements should translate to profits—that's after all what we are trying to improve. One company routinely reported cost savings from engineering improvements in excess of $5 million per year. Not once did we see anything close to such an impact on the company's profits. How we measured and tracked improvement was out of alignment with the goal.

- *End of the month hockey stick* Have you ever noticed at the end of the month (or quarter, or year) we ship a disproportionately large amount of our sales? Unless your orders are all skewed to the last week of the month, this is a sure sign of misalignment. Something is out whack if you cannot ship consistently through the month, and can somehow pull it out at the end.

- *Mismatch between supply and demand* This is prevalent in companies selling out of stock; too much of some items, while at the same time not enough of others. This is a clear-cut case of misalignment.

Recognizing Low Engagement

A different set of symptoms will be evident when a company needs to increase engagement. In teams lacking engagement, the evidence is best seen in the people themselves and how they approach their work. Some common symptoms to look for include:

- *Are people generating ideas or waiting to be told what to do?* Engaged people are solving problems all the time, even before they occur. At a minimum they are making efforts and taking action.

- *People give explanations of why something happened, not what they are doing about it* A friend of mine and amazing consultant, Ravi Gilani, has a saying he uses frequently, "Reasonable reasons + job not done = job not done." When engagement is lacking, people don't feel ownership for solving a problem so they spend their time in explanations.

- *Blame* Lack of engagement will almost always lead to blaming. When people are not engaged in our work and motivated to find better ways blaming is about all that is left for them to do. Engaged teams don't spend much time on blame, they figure out what they can do about it.

- *People keep to regular hours* I am not an advocate of working people long hours, and it should be everyone's goal to achieve more in fewer hours. But more often than not, when people come in at 9 and leave at 5, it means they are not highly engaged in the work. Engaged people often come in early or stay late until something important gets done.

If you see signs like these, you should be focusing your efforts on increasing engagement in your company.

You will undoubtedly see opportunities for improving both Alignment and Engagement in your company. Pinpoint as best you can which component needs work. If people are working their tails off and striving to solve problems, you are not likely to see much of a gain by trying to increase engagement. Clearly there must be some misalignment blocking such a group from producing greater results. Don't be surprised to find one part of your business suffers more from mis-alignment, while in another better engagement is the concern. Adapt your efforts as needed. Any time you find your continued efforts are producing diminishing returns, take it as a cue to re-evaluate your focus. If you want your efforts to have the maximum bottom line return, be sensitive to the symptoms discussed above. Then focus on the proper issue.

Getting the Most from these Practices

Understanding the distinct roles Alignment and Engagement play will keep you on track and moving forward. Every great sports coach knows sometimes you need to inspire your players (engagement) and sometimes you need to adjust your game plan (alignment).

The practices provided to create your successful team are divided into two sections: practices to improve alignment and practices to improve engagement. The practices are all created as stand-alone activities delivering benefits whether you implement one or many of them. At the beginning of each practice you'll see the Profit Boosters for monitoring results and maximizing returns. Some practices will undoubtedly fall more easily into your comfort zone and those can be great places to start. Please keep in mind, getting outside your comfort zone will likely offer the greatest opportunity to you; because these are the activities you are probably least inclined to do today. Consequently, they are more likely to be the missing elements your team needs most.

The criteria in selecting the practices I included here was not so much novelty, as effectiveness. They were selected from my experiences of more than 25 years in consulting and supporting my clients around the world. Every practice selected for the book has been used with great results in many places and by leaders from a range of different types of businesses. Some practices will strike you as common sense or resemble wisdom you have seen work in the past. Practical wisdom comes from many sources and I am grateful to all of the mentors, clients, colleagues, friends, and great managers I have had the good fortune to know for the contributions that have come together to produce these practices.

The most important thing you can do is to act. When you find something appealing, go out and put it into practice, try it, use it, test it. Do it for a couple of weeks. This is the only way you will get any real value from the book. And keep in mind it is a process and that is why I call it a practice. As you do it over and over again you will get better at it and your results will grow. This is not a crash diet to lose 25 pounds, it's a journey to become the leader you want to be and have the great company and career you deserve.

Having engaged and motivated teams is necessary to the lasting and growing success of any business. Being the leader who facilitates and fosters success is one of the more rewarding experiences you can enjoy. You can create a lasting positive impact on your employees and their families, your customers, your community and of course yourself. It's a great journey and one well worth taking. I wish you great success and all the rewards that come with it.

Chapter 4

Practices for Alignment

"Teamwork is the ability to work together toward a common vision; the ability to direct individual accomplishments toward organizational objectives. It is the fuel that allows common people to attain uncommon results."   *-Andrew Carnegie*

As we've already said, a great team is a winning team; a team achieving its goals. In business, winning means making more and more money, now and in the future—the goal of for-profit companies. We understand this so well, yet sometimes we gloss over it and miss its full implications. Let's understand what it really means and how companies are really performing toward this goal.

Most companies achieve profits, or they don't stick around for very long. Maybe your company is profitable right now, and it almost certainly has been in the past. The goal of companies is not just to make money; it's to make *more and more money* both now and in the future.

This means more than just being profitable. It means we are **increasing profits** over time—quarter to quarter, year to year. Very few companies are able to achieved sustained growth like this. Clearly, there is room for improvement. As in other endeavors, creating a great team in business is not a very common thing   at all.

"Making Money" as the Goal

Before we dive into the critical subject of alignment, it's worth taking a moment to talk about the value and limitations of using money as a company's goal. As with every goal we set, there are also important necessary conditions that must be met along the way. You may want to achieve a certain weight loss, but you aren't going to starve yourself to get there—so you intuitively set a necessary condition of continuing to eat regular meals each day. In our businesses there are many necessary conditions as well that need to be met as we pursue the goal of making money. Your business will have its own list, but there are two that tend to be common to every company:

- We must satisfy our customers

- We must satisfy our employees

Ignoring these conditions may make you more money in the immediate near term, but if you ignore them for long they will come back to bite you. Fortunately, achieving these conditions is very well aligned with the goal of making money. We know happy customers are key to the success and growth of the company and we put much energy into achieving it. You may not be aware that research shows that the same is true for our employees. Forbes Magazine reported in 2014 that the companies on their list of the "100 Best Companies to Work For" increased revenues by more than 22% on average.[1] There's little doubt having happy engaged employees goes hand in hand with increasing profits.

Making more and more money is the goal of the company, and for most of us, our motivation goes beyond making money. Even Gordon Gekko, the epitome of the greed mentality from the **Wall Street** movies, admits "It's not about the money. It's about the game between people."[2]

It's absolutely acceptable to communicate a larger mission of the company to your people and to use it to inspire, align and engage them. Money, is a great way to keep score, and it's important to keep that score front and center. It is the way the investors and owners evaluate performance. For simplicity's sake, I will speak to the goal in terms of making money, or profit in this book.

The Importance of Alignment

Change might be the only certainty we can rely on—market preferences shift, technology evolves, economies go through cycles, the competitive landscape changes, and a host of other factors. Making more and more money over time requires a team to adapt and adjust to these changes, in order to stay aligned together but adapting to the shifting needs of the business.

You have probably seen a flock of birds, or a school of fish responding to a change in the wind or current, or reacting to a predator. Each animal alters its course relative to the rest to keep the entire group together and moving forward as one toward its destination. Similarly, the more we can keep our company aligned and working cooperatively in the face of change and threat, the better our performance will be.

Creating alignment is one of the more challenging roles a leader must play. The frequency of the use of the term "silos," attests to how difficult it is. Alignment is one of the critical components of effective execution. The best strategy in the world is useless if the company cannot execute it. And execution is as much about getting your organized aligned and working together as it is anything else. So difficult though they may be, efforts to improve alignment will pay handsome dividends in performance.

The practices in the rest of this chapter are all designed to help you improve alignment in your company. Tackling such a big issue can seem daunting. In reality it is like most things, if you take it one step at a time. You can make progress before you know it. As you read the practices here, I encourage you to start using them in your daily routine. You don't have to tackle them all together or wait until you have completed reading the book. If you see one you like, do it. Each step you take will give you more momentum and move you further down the road to a more profitable and rewarding business.

Practice 1:
Communicate The Goal

This may sound like a simple, even trivial practice, but it works because of a simple principle we all understand very well—"out of sight, out of mind." We can know something intellectually, but when it is not front and center in the top of our mind, it is easy to lose sight of it. And in business this happens frequently because there is so much "noise," so many distractions, fires to fight, and daily tasks to perform that it is very easy to lose track of why we are doing them.

This is particularly true as you move downward in the company. The owners and top-management spend most of their day thinking about the goal and how to get more of it. Their measurements generally revolve around the goal or are closely linked to it and even they can get distracted from it by the numerous urgent demands of the day. As you go lower in the organization, people only get more and more remote from the goal. The production supervisor is focused on keeping his machines running, or making quality parts. The customer service rep is busy solving customer concerns and addressing technical problems. These are all important and all connected to the goal, to be sure. But if making more money is not top of mind decisions can easily get out of alignment with the goal.

Remember, people want to be connected to a larger purpose—they want to be part of a great team. Articulating and frequently communicating the goal reminds everyone on why we are doing what we are doing. You will find when the goal is front and center, people will make better decisions to align themselves with the goal and with each other.

Some leaders may fear that talking about the goal of "making more and more money," will alienate their team because it is about the owners or management getting rich. Creating a purpose you think people will rally better around is a great thing. Giving people a sense of mission around making money will surely help them connect to the company and their colleagues. They will be more likely to pull together and work together to get there. At the same time don't be shy about presenting the importance of making money as the way to keep score. Growing profits is the critical result that enables everything else to happen. Without that there is no vehicle to pursue anything else.

Here are a couple of different things you can do to communicate the goal in a very constructive way, no matter where you think your team is. First of all, understand your people already know the goal is to make money. You can ask them, "Assume you were the owner of the business and tell me, what is the goal of the company, and why does it exist?" Overwhelmingly they will tell you, it is to make money.

Additionally, there are at least two critical conditions to meet or the company will not achieve the goal of making more and more money over time. The first is we must make our customers happy. If we do not provide them with the right products, service and prices, they will not buy and we will not have a successful company. The second condition is we must make all our employees happy. If we do not provide them sufficient earnings, challenges, opportunities and a good working environment, they will not produce their best work or even worse will leave the company. You cannot reach the goal without both of these.

In the end all three elements are required—making money, having satisfied customers, and taking care of your team. As long as you keep sight of these elements, you are free to choose how to communicate your company's goal to your people in the most constructive way. You can emphasize the value your product brings to your customers, how the service you offer frees people from drudgery, how producing your product at a lower cost enables more people to acquire and enjoy it, etc. But whatever you do, talk about it, keep the goal front and center.

Without a strong connection to the ultimate purpose the company is fulfilling work becomes just that...work. And more importantly without a common goal connecting everyone, alignment is simply not possible.

When the goal (in all three of its critical aspects—making money, satisfying customers, and treating employees well) is always top of mind you will find that people work more collaboratively and more constructively. The goal is the "North Star" everyone steers by.

Profit Booster Tips:

- ✓ When ideas are presented in meetings, ask how they will impact the goal
- ✓ Remind people frequently of how their job contributes to profits and customer satisfaction
- ✓ Ask people where they think their efforts can contribute most to the goal

Practice 2:
Share Company Results with Everyone

Sharing how the company is performing is critical to creating alignment in your team. For people to be connected to your goal, they need to know how well they are doing in terms of it. You wouldn't hide the score of the soccer game from your team, so don't hide your company's performance either.

Providing periodic financial results gives critical feedback information to your team and reinforces the goal of making more money. Many leaders already do this, as a matter of course. It helps everyone to know if we are getting better, stuck on a plateau, or going in the wrong direction. You don't have to post a full financial statement or try to make every employee into a CPA. Select a few summary measures you feel are a good reflection of the total picture and post them each accounting period. Using a trend chart to show the picture over time is even better. Making a million dollars profit may sound pretty good, but if we made ten million the previous month, we are heading in the wrong direction. Show a chart so anyone, and everyone, can see at a glance which direction we are going.

Showing the company results is great for reinforcing alignment—we are all in it together, working toward one common goal. Just taking this action will increase people's connection to the goal and remind them in the end, the measure that matters most is the bottom line, not my local department's metrics.

If you want to go further than the profit and loss statement, I suggest keeping the measures to a minimum, focused around a few key strategic issues that drive profits and business growth. Things like: "same store sales," "on-time deliveries," "new accounts," "first time right quality," and "customer returns," are examples of "team-level" metrics. These measures keep people focused on the big picture and help connect performance to things they can impact directly. Going into a large number of departmental metrics when talking about company performance usually serves to disconnect people from the goal and from each other. Be careful to select measures that cut across departments and where there is a clear and obvious connection to the goal.

Many managers also feel the need to add explanations to the results, like, "Profits went up last month due to our successful efforts to increase selling prices to a number of large customers." Such explanations can be useful in helping people to interpret and understand the results, which is a good thing. However, attributing the results to a couple of specific causes can send the signal the contributions of other areas were not as important. Be careful, it may divide your team. In the end we succeed or fail together, so creating and maintaining alignment is critical. If you do feel the need to explain the results, do it carefully making sure not to create heroes and villains in the process.

Profit Booster Tips:

- ✓ Present results in a simple format—charts showing trends on key metrics work best
- ✓ Focus on a small number of global strategic indicators vs. pages of KPI's to promote alignment
- ✓ Consider how people might interpret your explanations before you present them

Practice 3:
Replace Local Measures with Global Ones

Global measures—those relating to the overall performance of the company—should be the main focus of every business. But it is difficult to use top-level measures like Net Profit, and ROI to evaluate the performance of people in individual departments of the company who do not have a large degree of control over those results. This leads to a tendency to devise and use local or departmental measures to monitor and motivate the performance of people in those areas. It's certainly easier to measure individual performance and accountability when the individual can largely control the measure being used. However, devising measures that are controllable at the local level AND aligned with taking the right actions to improve company performance, is a difficult undertaking. If you are not careful, the local measures can result in actions producing unintended outcomes.

Many local measures are based on cost—saving operating expense. Cost is relatively easy to assign to a person or department, so many departmental measures are cost-based. Focusing people on cost, particularly local costs, over which they have much control, often results in efforts to save money and creates problems in other parts of the business. For example, when purchasing finds an item for a lower price, but has to buy a 12-month supply in order to get the discount. Six months later if Engineering changes the design, they may have to scrap half a year's supply of those "cheap goods."

Local measures can also drive people to compartmentalize their job. They define their role in terms of the objectives set for their department and lose sight of the company goal and performance. If the departmental measures are driven too hard in the company, it will not take long until people define their job according to the local measures. Instead of thinking in terms of how to make the company succeed, they will focus on "doing their job," and maximizing their local performance measures. This can be devastating to alignment and wall people off into the "silos" occurring all too often on companies.

Instead, shift the focus back to the global measures—Net Profit and ROI and their components, Throughput, Investment and Operating Expense. You don't have to get rid of your current local measures, especially at first. Bringing people back to the big picture, making money, and by putting company-level measurements first, is essential. It's equivalent to telling an athletic team—the score on the scoreboard is what matters most. The goal of measurements in a company is less to have accountability, and more to help the company be as successful as possible.

I suggest you worry less about how to assign individual responsibility for results. Everyone should be responsible for trying to reach the goal. Put your global measures front and center and be careful of local measures that can drive people into silos and disconnect them from the goal. People can handle the ambiguity. After all it's a lot better to be aiming approximately in the right direction, than precisely in the wrong one.

Profit Booster Tips

- ✓ Always list company measures above department measures
- ✓ Talk about company measures first
- ✓ If local measures look good and the company performance isn't, something is amiss with your metrics, look into it!

Practice 4:
Find the Constraint of Your Business

If sharing financial performance is something many companies already do, identifying the company's constraint is a practice that all too few have done. Constraints exist in every company, and knowing yours is a huge advantage in growing your profits. Since the term 'constraint' is used in different ways it often has widely differing meanings, so let me clarify what I mean when I use the word and why it's so critical to your results.

One helpful analogy is to think of your business as a series of interconnected 'pipes.' In order to sell, produce and deliver your product or service work must pass through a series of steps, or pipes. The amount of work flowing through each length of pipe is dependent on the capacity of each segment. Less work will flow through small diameter (capacity) pipes than through larger pipes which have more capacity. The output of the entire system of pipes will be determined by the smallest segment of pipe in your system—the department or resource with the least capacity. If you increase the capacity of one of the larger pipes, you won't get any more total output from your pipeline, because work will simply back up at the one with the least capacity.

The chain analogy is helpful in understanding the importance of finding their constraint is to think of your business as a chain. In order to deliver your product or service and generating revenues, you need every link in your chain to do its job effectively. We all know every chain is only as strong as its weakest link—the constraint. The weakest link, or smallest segment of pipe is the constraint of your business. If you want to produce more revenues and profits, it's critical to know where your constraint is. If you are delivering every order you have on time and in full, the constraint will likely be in sales, because clearly you have the capacity to fulfill all the orders you have. If you are unable to meet all of your orders on time, or are turning away or pushing out orders, then your constraint is somewhere inside your operations. Knowing your constraint is critical to better performance.

One of the greatest things about this realization is it means you can make significant gains by just focusing on and improving the constraint. There aren't a hundred constraints in your business, or even ten. It's probably not more than two or three at the most. If you widen the smallest segment of pipe, or strength the weakest link in your chain, the entire system (your company) produces more revenue. You will continue to see revenues grow until the improvements have increased the capacity of that area so much, it is no longer the constraint. Again, knowing your constraint is critical to better performance.

When you don't know where your constraint is, people don't know where to put their efforts. Usually this means efforts are scattered and diffused all across the business. In other words, people are busy strengthening already stronger links in the chain or widening pipes other than the narrowest. This means people's efforts are out of alignment with what the business needs most to improve its performance. It also means the vast majority of people's efforts will have little or no real impact on the business. This can quickly create dis-engagement as well, because when people work very hard to improve something and we cannot see any significant result from it, they get discouraged.

By finding your constraint, you can change this quickly and drive results much faster than most people imagine is possible. If the constraint is internal within your supply chain going a little further to pinpoint the department, function or even the process that most limits you will enable you to direct your team to the most critical opportunities. One simple way to identify your constraint is to look for where work has backed up the most. Just as a long line of cars forms behind an accident on the highway or ahead of a construction zone, you will see the same symptoms at your constraint. So look for the biggest piles of work, or the places where things get stuck the most as they move through your business. Improving these areas will increase the flow enabling you to produce and ship more orders and grow your profits.

Just the simple knowledge of where the constraint is will cause people to take actions to improve it. Here are a couple of additional steps that will give you even more leverage for improvement.

1. *Communicate the location of the constraint to everyone, not just those in the constraint area.* Often great solutions come from outside of the constraint area when people find ways to help the constraint get more accomplished. Think of a doctor's office where the capacity of the doctor to diagnose and treat patients is typically the constraint. By having nurses or technician's prep patients for the doctor and pull the files needed, the doctor is able to see more patients.

2. *Just start!* Often people struggle to agree on what is their constraint and leaders have confessed they got stuck due to concern about misidentifying their constraint. Don't worry, if you have narrowed it down to a couple of potential areas, that's terrific. Already this means you have sharpened the focus of your company and it's not uncommon to have a couple of areas that are very close to being constraints. Just pick one and improve it. When you think it's no longer the most limiting resource, move to the next.

3. *Pay attention to revenues.* The best way to tell if you are working on the constraint is to monitor your revenues or output. When you increase the capacity of the smallest segment of pipe, the output of the whole system of pipes increases. If your improvements continue to increase revenues at the end of the pipes, that area is still the constraint. As soon as your improvement efforts stop showing an increase in revenues at the end, then the constraint has likely moved and it's time to adjust and re-focus.

If you follow this practice you will see rapid increases in your revenues. Rather than having to make improvements in many places across your operation, your focused efforts on the constraint will quickly result in higher revenues. In teaching this practice to companies over the last 25 years improvements of 15-20% in revenues is quite common, just from addressing the first constraint you find. Repeating the practice as the constraint moves to other areas enables you to continue to accelerate your results. Most of my clients who have taken this practice heart see gains of 30-100% in less than a year. So make finding your constraint a regular practice and accelerate your results.

Profit Booster Tips

- ✓ Look for where work piles up to find the constraint
- ✓ Ask your expediters where things are usually stuck
- ✓ Let everyone know the constraint
- ✓ Use measures to call attention to the constraint and monitor improvement
- ✓ Don't communicate the constraint is the result of poor performance
- ✓ Usually something becomes a constraint because getting more of it is difficult or expensive. Often one of your most skilled resources will be your constraint, because it is more rare and harder to develop or purchase.

Practice 5:
Blue Light Your Business
🕐🎯

Every company has bottlenecks which jeopardize deliveries and limit growth. Breaking them can be costly, time consuming and risky, especially if you are making a capital investment to do it. Aligning your team to recognize and address these bottlenecks exposes hidden opportunities that can typically increase the bottleneck's output 25% or more with little or no cost.

The term Blue Light comes from one of the first projects I ever did as a consultant to business leaders. You can read the full story on my blog www.myviablevision.com/blog/bluelight. The short version of the story is my client had a bottleneck they were struggling with. It was in the welding department on the factory floor and it was holding up shipments and disrupting client relationships. After an initial analysis we applied the "What good looks like," practice (Practice 8) to create a simple image of what should be happening in the welding department. What we came up with was the image of "Blue Light"—the welding torches should be fired up and welding. This simple image enabled them to realize there was a lot of time that the welders were busy, but not welding.

They observed a number of activities that 'interfered' with the welders welding—the Blue Light. They found fast, simple and virtually free ways to address these 'interferences' which enabled them to increase the output of the bottleneck more than 50% in a matter of weeks. This not only saved them the cost of expanding their facility and of hiring and training more welders, but it increased their shipments almost immediately, instead of the 4-5 months that new construction and training would have taken.

As with any bottleneck you can throw money at it—overtime, another shift, more people, outsourcing, etc. Doing this as a first step tends to create a culture of spending and doesn't motivate people to think in innovative ways to find better solutions. And very often, "the throw money at the problem," approach doesn't offer a fast solution. How long does it take to find, hire and train a new machinist, or engineer, or designer? It's not going to happen today, or even tomorrow. So the problem is going to persist for a while.

The Blue Light practice will help you expose and capitalize on hidden capacity in your business. You can use it on any resource where you need to increase output. The Interference Chart at the end of the practice is a great tool to guide you and engage your team in the process.

1. Define the "Blue Light," of the resource you need more out of. This is the core work, skill or capability to accomplish the job at that step of your process. It is the work requiring the level of skill or capability of the resource. As an example, imagine a doctor's office. The blue light of the doctor is "diagnosing and treating the patients," the work needing to be done and which requires the doctor's level of capability.

2. Find a way to observe and measure how much of the resource's time is doing the Blue Light work. I am fond of the simple, direct approach. Go several times a day and count how many of the critical resources are doing the Blue Light work when you observe. Visiting several times over a day or two will give you a pretty good idea of your Blue Light time—and how much hidden capacity is available.

3. Identify and address anything preventing you from keeping the Blue Light on. Simple observation (or more formal data collection) and analysis of the resource will indicate where you are losing your Blue Light time, and point you in the direction of your solutions. Streamlining, eliminating, or offloading those activities will enable your bottleneck to do more of what only it

can do. And by opening up its capacity you will ship more and increase revenues and customer satisfaction.

4. Use the Interference Chart to structure the process. Write the Blue Light activity of your bottleneck in the center circle as show below. Then create as many circles as you need around the perimeter to capture all of the things that interfere or take the bottleneck resource away from doing the Blue Light. (The Chart contains some of the actual observations my client noted in his welding department.) If you want you can add some estimates or calculated durations for how much time is lost to each of these interferences to further identify the critical areas to work on.

Interference Chart

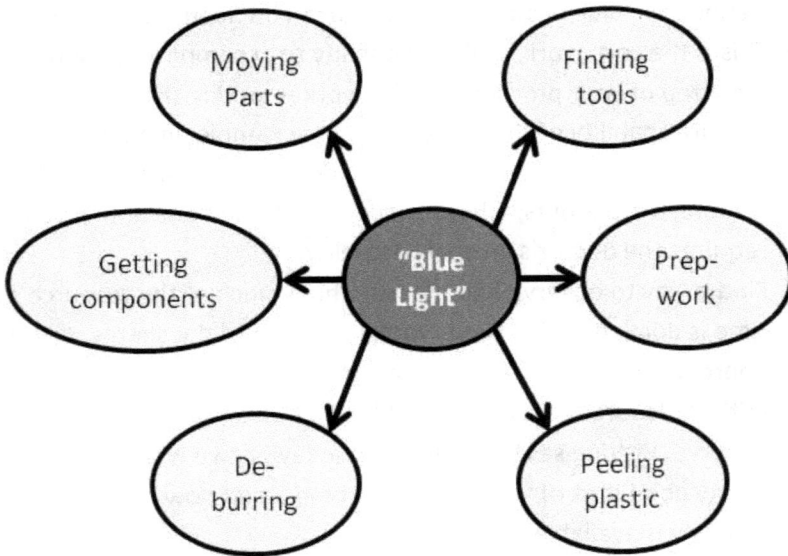

Moving Parts

Finding tools

Getting components

"Blue Light"

Prep-work

De-burring

Peeling plastic

I have shared this practice with thousands of managers over the past 20 years and the feedback I get is amazing. Almost everyone is shocked at just how much more capacity can be exposed with small, low-cost changes to how they work—20% is routine, and many report 50% more output by doing the Blue Light practice. It's been used on the factory floor, in the offices of doctors and lawyers, in pharmaceutical labs, with NASA Scientists, computer programmers, field technicians, across an array of government agencies, etc. and it never fails to produce results. Do it yourself at least once, so you can experience it first-hand. Once you grasp the magnitude of the opportunity, you'll want to teach to everyone in your business. Whenever people come asking for more people, additional equipment, or capital appropriations, you can ask them if they have "Blue Light-ed," (yes, it's a verb too!) the area, before you go and increase costs or investment.

Profit Booster Tips

- ✓ Look for backlogs of work to identify bottlenecks
- ✓ Do your own observations to see how much "blue light" there is
- ✓ Post a list of the interferences for all to see
- ✓ Ask people "what can we do about it, today?," to focus them on immediate fixes
- ✓ Don't accept solutions requiring time or investment as a first step

Practice 6:
Use T, I and OE to Align Decisions with the Goal

If you have read Eli Goldratt's bestseller, *The Goal*, you are already familiar with Throughput, Investment and Operating Expense—T, I, and OE. They offer a way to greatly simplify and more closely align decision making with the company's goal of making more money. This practice will get you and your people thinking more clearly about how their decisions impact company results.

As you move downward in the company pyramid, people get further from the financial outcomes and more involved in the "doing" of the work to produce those financial results. It is more difficult to judge how local actions will impact the goal, and this is where T, I, OE comes in.

Throughput (T) is the rate at which the company generates revenue through sales. It's the money the company gets from delivering its product or service. We want Throughput to go up.

Investment (I) is all the money the company invests in things it intends to sell. This includes all of the inventory you are holding as well as all your capital investments. We want to be able to generate Throughput with as little investment as possible, so we want I to go down.

Operating Expense (OE) is all the money we spend in turning inventory into Throughput. We want to drive this down.

T, I, OE simplifies the complexity of corporate accounting so anyone can quickly understand the basic elements. The measures tie directly to the bottom line so you reduce the distortions and confusion introduced by like "product cost."

Net Profit (NP) is equal to Throughput minus Operating Expense or

$$NP = T - OE$$

Return on Investment is just Profit divided by Investment or T − OE/ I

For any decision to lead to higher profits for the company the net impact of all three measures must be positive. So to evaluate any decision we need to consider how it will change each of the measures— T, I, OE. If the net impact is positive it's a good decision financially, if not it isn't.

Like most of the practices here, this will take some time to build people's skill and linking better decisions to the bottom line impact is critical to every business's success. Here's how you can start:

1. Inform people about the three metrics. Give them a quick primer in a staff meeting, or production meeting. Provide the definitions and a simple explanation. Close with telling them we want the net impact on T, I, OE to be positive.
2. Whenever there is a request for money (spending or investment) ask people to provide a T, I, OE analysis of the decision. This was a significant activity I was asked to do in my first job in industry in the late 1980's. These analyses I did stopped the company from spending hundreds of thousands of dollars that would have had a negative impact on T,I, OE, but which looked favorable using the old approval calculations. Additionally, it caused several highly profitable expenditures to be fast-tracked reaping more than a million dollars in increased profits.
3. Incorporate T, I, OE into your regular reviews and planning sessions. Ask people to share their plans for improving T, I, OE. Quiz them on what they did yesterday or last month, and plan to do tomorrow and this month to improve T, I, OE. At first this will be a challenge for people because many are not used to

thinking this way but it won't take long until they come with better responses and better decisions.

4. Post the results of actions or improvements showing the impact on T, I, OE and a brief explanation of the idea. "A second helper was added to the load station at a cost of $2,600 per month, resulting in increased Throughput shipments of $8,500 per month—a net gain of $5,900!" People will see what matters to the leadership and understand better how they can contribute.

T, I, and OE are common sense measurements virtually everyone can grasp quickly. It will take some time to get them used to applying them and incorporating them into their thinking and decisions-making. Keep at it, keep reminding and asking, and pretty soon this practice will yield real results. All it takes is a little effort on your part, which will pay off handsomely if you can get even one good solution or block one poor one.

Profit Booster Tips

- ✓ Get in the habit of asking how every change will impact T, I, OE
- ✓ Include T, I, OE in every formal analysis of larger investments or more significant changes
- ✓ Pay close attention to Throughput—improvements in one area do not always result in more revenues

Practice 7: Routinely Review and Re-Align Your Measures

"Tell me how you measure me and I will tell you how I will behave." Measurements are a very powerful force in influencing decisions and behavior. People will take act in ways to maximize the measurements we put upon them. Whether the measures are numeric and formal, or more informal, like what we always inquire about in meetings, or chastise people for doing, we are communicating the behavior we want in the business.

The measurements we use should promote alignment in our company—both with the goal and the rest of the company. Finding the right measures to drive the best performance and results is not a trivial thing, especially as the company grows larger and more complex. The fundamental problem is people work within sub-systems of your business—departments, functions, etc. The performance of these sub-systems is critical to the performance of your business, but they are only one of the contributing roles and factors in generating your profits. People within each sub-system only control performance within their area, and at the same time are impacted by decisions and actions taken by other sub-systems.

Manufacturing, for instance, can control certain things, like what they produce, the uptime of their machines, the processes they use to manufacture or assemble your products. If purchasing chooses to buy from an inexpensive but unreliable supplier because they are measured on the costs at which they buy goods, it will surely impact manufacturing's ability to deliver quality products on time. And the problem happens all over the organization, where achieving some local measure or objective, the things that group can control, has a negative impact on the overall performance of the company.

Fred Kofman, an executive at LinkedIn and former MIT professor highlights this conflict very effectively in a number of the entertaining videos he has produced.[3] His conclusion after years of researching the subject is there is not a way to fully solve this inherent problem, and I tend to agree with him. The key is to carefully monitor and adjust the local measures you use in order to promote *better* alignment. It will never be perfect, but perfect is probably beyond the reach of any of us in the first place, so finding better ways is more than sufficient to help us increase performance. Remember, conditions around and within your business are always changing, so regular review and adjustment of the measures you use is essential to creating better alignment across your business team.

The practice to do this involves looking at your company department by department and asking some fundamental questions. For each one you will want to put yourself in the shoes of the person or group operating under that measure. You can do this activity yourself for your direct reports and then ask them to continue the process within their department or work with them to do it.

1. Begin by listing the measurement(s), both the formal ones and the other things that you use to evaluate your team and the various departments or functions. If you have many measurements try to hone in on the ones that are used the most or which you see as most important. There are almost always 1-2 dominant measures that will be responsible for driving how people behave. Focus on these.

2. Ask yourself, "What is the best and easiest way for me to make these measures look as good as possible?" It's important to think in terms of the easiest way as part of this because people will always take the path of least resistance, even if they don't think through it quite as overtly as we are doing. List the actions and decisions someone in that position would make based on the situations they are in every day.

3. The second helpful question is: "Is there some way to make my local measurement look good that can hurt or hinder the company's performance, or cause problems for another part of the business?" Here you want to list possible actions or decisions that people might take under the measurement that create either mis-alignment with the goal, or mis-alignment with the rest of the company. You can then go and check to see if these things are indeed happening, if it isn't readily apparent.

4. Lastly, ask, "Does this measurement motivate me to do ALL the things I would want from that person or department to maximize our performance as a company?" Here you want to check not so much if the measures create misalignment, but if they are missing opportunities to create better alignment. List all the good things you want people in that department to do that are not being motivated by the current measures.

Doing such a review of your measurements will highlight where you have misalignments and also where there are opportunities to improve alignment with your company. You can then modify or supplement your existing measures or replace them entirely with new ones if you feel it's necessary. If you haven't done this in a while, you will almost certainly find misalignments you can correct. Don't be surprised or upset if you find a good bit of misalignment. If you have a lot of misalignment it means you will get even more of a jump in results by improving it.

Making this a regular practice will keep your business working together better and more aligned to reaching your goal.

Profit Booster Tips

- ✓ List the biggest challenges in your business and ask how your measures are contributing to them
- ✓ Ask yourself if there is a way to maximize a local measure but hurt the company in the process—it could be occurring

- ✓ Assume the role of devil's advocate—it's better to speculate about problems that might not exist, than to overlook misalignments for lack of investigation
- ✓ Use T, I, OE to determine how local measures impact profits
- ✓ Look downstream for problems that could be caused by departmental measures

Practice 8:
Map What Good Alignment Looks Like
⊚✦➕

Alignment is all about coordination—how the individual people and parts of your team work together to produce the result. Too often our businesses operate in 'silos' *as if* they are separate, almost unrelated entities. To be truly effective in reaching the goal, you need to get them to work as one.

Because the silo mentality is so strong, people often don't know how they relate to or impact the departments around them, or sometimes even the person at the desk next to them. This practice will help you provide a simple picture of what good alignment looks like and improve the coordination in your business.

1. Draw a simple flowchart of your business, or any sub-process where you want to improve alignment. Use circles and arrows to describe the activities and relationships. I suggest drawing things at a level of detail where it will fit legibly on a single page. Keeping your picture to one page ensures people don't lose sight of the big picture. Here's an example of a chart from a doctor's office.

Doctor's Office Workflow Chart

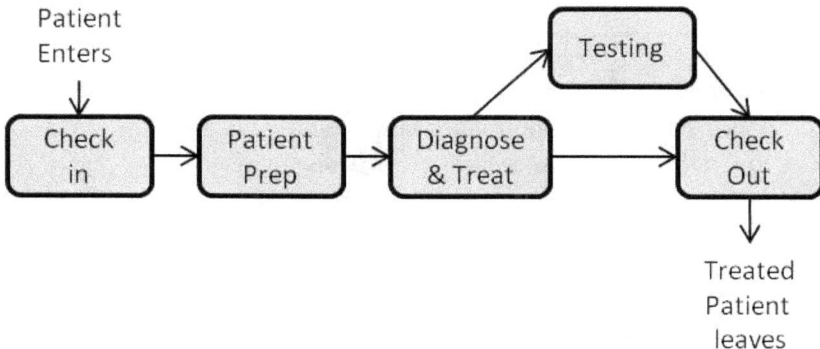

Patient
Enters

Check in → Patient Prep → Diagnose & Treat → Testing → Check Out

Treated Patient leaves

2. Create one or two simple statements to communicate "what good looks like" for each of the process steps you have put on your diagram. Don't try to capture everything, just the essence of what one would 'see' if that step were doing its job effectively, right now. For the doctor's office example, we would want the doctor to be "diagnosing and treating patients as much as possible"—not doing other things that could be done by a nurse or assistant. This also drives how all the other parts of the business *should* work together.

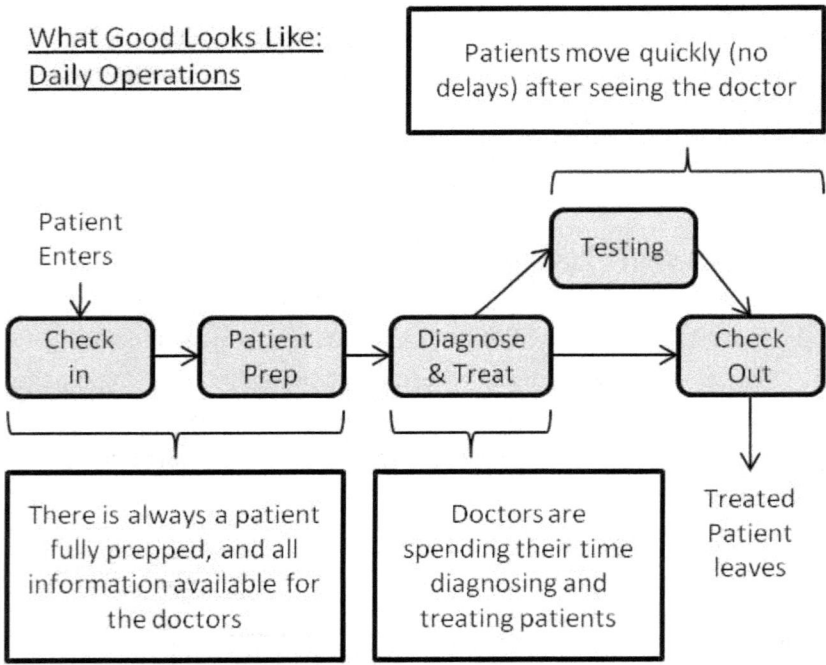

What Good Looks Like:
Daily Operations

Patients move quickly (no delays) after seeing the doctor

Patient Enters

Testing

Check in → Patient Prep → Diagnose & Treat → Check Out

There is always a patient fully prepped, and all information available for the doctors

Doctors are spending their time diagnosing and treating patients

Treated Patient leaves

3. To enhance the impact of the alignment map you can add one more statements about each step—what *improvement* looks like. To be more and more effective we need to get people not just to perform their daily tasks well, but to engage them in improving those processes too. Should they try to do their activity faster, at a lower cost, more consistently, in more depth, more expansively, etc.? Adding a simple statement to communicate the improvement people should be striving for

will further enhance alignment. In the doctor's office example below I am showing only what improvement looks like for each step. On your diagram you will want to show also the statement you wrote for step 2.

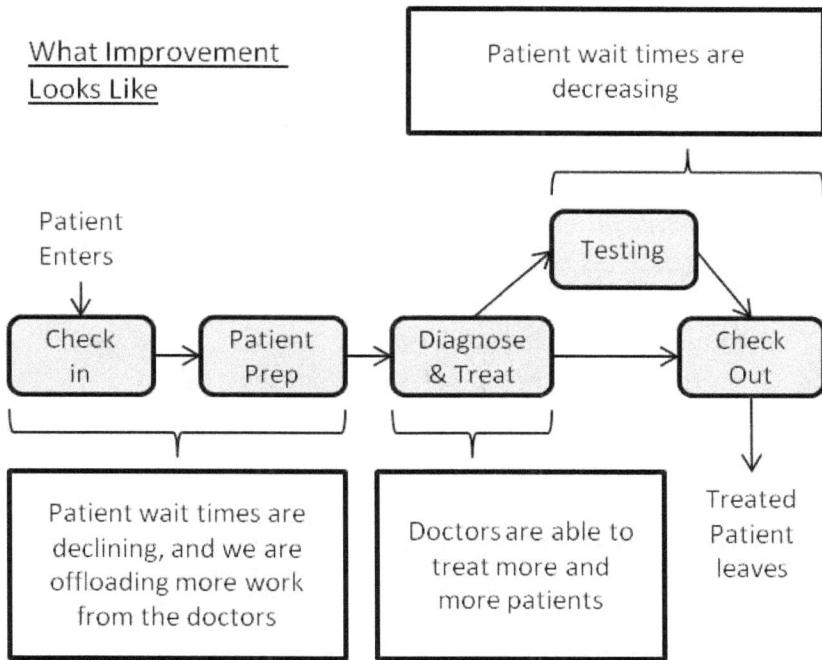

What Improvement
Looks Like

| | Patient wait times are decreasing |

Patient
Enters

| Check in | → | Patient Prep | → | Diagnose & Treat | → | Testing | → | Check Out |

Patient wait times are declining, and we are offloading more work from the doctors

Doctors are able to treat more and more patients

Treated
Patient
leaves

4. Share the picture of what good looks like with your team. My clients frequently post these pictures around the department or business as a way to communicate and keep 'what good looks like' top-of-mind for people. They also serve as a simple effective way for you to reinforce the right behaviors and actions. By referring people back to the map you help them improve their performance and you connect them to the template for repeating it in the future.

Defining 'what good looks like' is also highly effective for increasing engagement in your business, and there is a related practice in Chapter Five. It is extremely difficult and risky to try to script how things should be done in your business in order to get the results you want. By applying 'what good looks like' you give people the desired outcome you are seeking and freeing them up to find better and better ways of reaching it. This practice is part of a larger process I use to help companies align their organization with their business strategy, called The Throughput Operating Strategy (TOS). If you want additional information on this methodology you can find it at www.myviablevision.com.

Profit Booster Tips

- ✓ Use your flowchart to train and educate new employees on how you do business as a team. They may know the technical part of their jobs from a previous employer, but the teamwork process is probably unique to your business
- ✓ Ask people to use the map of 'what good looks like' as a template, comparing that picture with what is actually happening during the work day. Whenever they see a gap it's time to take corrective action.
- ✓ Refer to the flowchart until it is engrained in people's heads and they are operating consistently according to it
- ✓ 'Less is more' when creating the statements for what good looks like. Prescribing detailed solutions almost never works. By keeping your statements open-ended you are providing the essential criteria people should use in making decisions and seeking improvements.

Practice 9:
Spend Most of Your Time and Energy on Today
🕐⊙🎯

As far as I know there is still no way to change yesterday. The only thing we can impact is today, what we do right now. In many of the companies I work with I find a large portion of management time is spent talking about what happened in the past. We analyze, we try to find why things happened, we review the numbers, we report on what has happened, we try to assign responsibility or blame. What's the point? The only thing we can do about yesterday is learn from it and do things better today.

Shifting your focus to today is enormously empowering and effective. For starters, when you focus most of your time working to make today successful you get much more done. You also eliminate all the wasted energy, ill-will, and blaming that re-living yesterday's mistakes and shortcomings creates. So here are some ways to practice focusing on today.

1. Never start a meeting with what happened yesterday. So many meetings start with a review of the past, this ensures that much of the meeting will be spent discussing things we can do nothing about. Yes, understanding the past is not unimportant, but it has become the central focus of so many companies that there is often no time left to deal with today.

2. Begin meetings with what we need to do today and focus on the obstacles to getting it done. When people are looking at what needs to happen they will see many of the obstacles they face at a point in time when we can actually do something about them.

3. Ask what we need to be successful today. We can anticipate many potential problems and with time we will learn what we need to check to uncover potential problems and risks. Are all the people I need going to show up for work today? Is the

equipment I need running properly? Do I have the parts, specs, sign-offs, etc.? Are my sales appointments confirmed? Are expectations for my upcoming sales calls clear and understood?

4. When you look at the past, focus on learning and corrective action. The past is not unimportant; it can and should be a great teacher. But it is only useful in how we change the present and future. So whenever you are reviewing the past ask people to come with solutions to prevent these things today and in the future, and limit explanations of why it happened. This only provokes the "cover-your-backside" response. Then spend most of the time on the way forward, not things we cannot change.

Practicing these steps will shift everyone's attention to corrective and preventive action. This is all you can do anyway and it is the only way to make your results better.

Profit Booster Tips

- ✓ Stop blaming with a simple question—"ok, but what can we do about it now?"
- ✓ Always ask what we can do to prevent a problem from happening again
- ✓ Use "we" instead of "you" or "I" to promote group problem solving
- ✓ Ask what you can do to help

Practice 10:
Use Pareto to Stop Wasting Efforts
🕐🎯

Eli Goldratt, one of my mentors, believed the biggest constraint in most companies is management attention. What people do in a business is the direct result of where management puts its attention, so what we choose to pay attention to is what the rest of the organization will do as well. Let's face it, we only have a limited amount of time so we cannot give the attention needed to everything that could be done to improve the business. We must choose. If we choose to push a large number of initiatives, spreading our efforts across many things, that is what our people will do. They will spread small portions of their time across many things.

We all know the Pareto principle: 20% of the things are responsible for 80% of the results. My experience dictates it's probably more like 5% of the things drive 95% of the results, but it doesn't matter, the lesson is the same. A small number of things will provide the majority of the benefits. Focusing on and accomplishing those things is by far more important than making a little bit of progress on everything that could improve your business.

Most people feel the key to doing this is finding the significant few, among the trivial many. This is not the problem at all, it's exactly the opposite. I'd be willing to bet you already know the most critical initiatives your company needs to be doing. And if you don't, it won't take you more than 10 minutes to think and list them. The real challenge in applying Pareto's Law, is stopping the multitude of less significant activities. This is where your attention gets drained and this is where your organization's efforts are getting wasted.

Here's a practice to help you pare away all the stuff that is sucking your precious resources and keeping your business from addressing its most important issues.

1. Make a list of the all the projects or initiatives your company or department is working on and put them in a rough priority sequence based on their impact on the bottom line, as well as their necessity from a "right to operate" standpoint.
2. Freeze the bottom 50% of the projects or initiatives. Yes, that's it, just stop them in their tracks so no one works on them anymore. Put them on hold until the projects above them are finished and they move into the top 50%.
3. Unfreeze projects as the more important ones get finished and the frozen ones move up in priority.
4. Whenever a new idea or project arises, pull out the list. Ask people where the new project fits on the list. If it falls in the top 50%, require that you freeze one of the active projects, or wait until one finishes, before starting the new project.
5. Spend the majority of your time focusing on the top projects. Whatever you pay attention to, so will your people. Spend enough time checking how people are spending their time to ensure that other projects are not draining your people away from the top ones.

To achieve a better focus in your company, set your sights on eliminating or stopping the less important projects. When people's attention is not distracted by all of the lesser things, they can devote their focus to the most important activities. Your results will take a quantum leap forward.

Profit Booster Tips

- ✓ Keep a list of the top 2-3 projects or initiatives
- ✓ Go to great lengths to ensure trivial projects are NOT being worked on (people rarely drop something they have invested time on easily)
- ✓ Ask people why they can't spend their entire day on the most important project

- ✓ Make it a habit to walk around and see what people are working on
- ✓ Set aside blocks of your day when you don't allow any interruptions

Practice 11:
Stop the Multi-Tasking
🕐➕

Multi-tasking is rampant in society and business. People are constantly setting aside one task they are working on, before it is completed to go and do something else. It has traditionally been viewed as a desirable skill or talent in people working in business. But every scientific study of multi-tasking and performance shows exactly the same results:

Multi-tasking reduces efficiency, increases the chance of errors, and delays the completion of work

All the research supports this fact. There are three things you need to know about multi-tasking to understand why you must address it in your business.

1. Whenever a task is set aside to do something else, efficiency will be lost and capacity wasted when the task is re-started. We don't automatically pick up where we left off with the same level of effectiveness as when we were engaged in it before. It takes time to get back up to speed, to get back into the material, to remember where you were and what exactly you were doing. The more complicated the task, the more time will typically be lost each time you re-start.

2. Multi-tasking greatly increases the likelihood of errors and quality problems. Software people have told me for the last 10 years that multi-tasking is probably the biggest cause of bugs in programs. It's not hard to believe either, because when you stop and re-start tasks it's easy to miss some little part of what you were doing and introduce an error.

3. Multi-tasking greatly extends the time it takes to complete work. Every time we someone stops one task to do something else, that task sits, doing nothing. When multi-tasking is widespread, as it often is, completing the task is less a function of the actual work, and more about the frequency and duration

of the interruptions. The diagram below shows an example where a person has three tasks to complete. Illustration A on top shows the time to complete the three tasks if they are worked one at a time until complete. Illustration B below it shows how completions times are extended when the person multi-tasks across the three projects, doing a little work on each until all are finished.

Multi-tasking Creates Delays

A. Three tasks worked one at a time to completion:

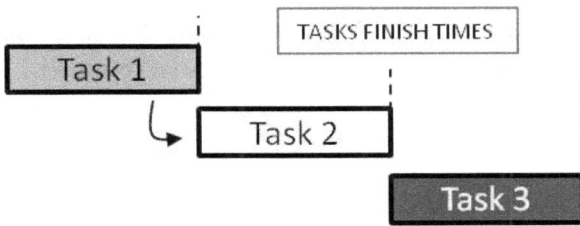

TASKS FINISH TIMES

Task 1

Task 2

Task 3

B. Same three tasks being worked a little at a time (multi-tasking):

ALL TASKS FINISH LATER

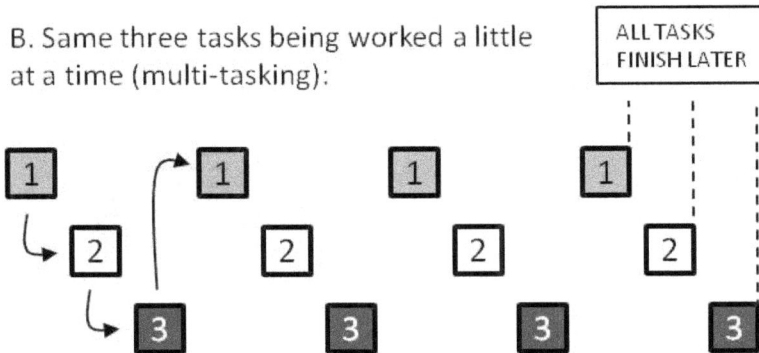

1   1   1   1

2   2   2   2

3   3   3   3

4. Notice that multi-tasking delays the completion of ALL the tasks—not just the last one in the sequence. And since Task 1 on the Gray project may just be one of many work steps that have to be completed, the delay caused by multi-tasking will delay when the next phase of work can be done. If that step multi-tasks in a similar way, it's not hard to see how delays can grow to many times the length of the actual work that needs to be done.

To greatly reduce the multi-tasking in your business, and increase efficiency, reduce errors and accelerate projects, try these activities:

1. Reduce the number of available tasks people to have on their plate at any one time. Usually a couple is enough to enable them to work efficiently if there is some natural downtime within a task.
2. Put all the emphasis on *finishing* tasks, not working on them.
3. Keep work in common pools and only hand out the next job to someone when they finish one from their desk. The diagram below shows the conventional approach of distributing work as soon as it arrives, which invites multi-tasking. On the following page the illustration shows how to pool work in a common queue and only release it as capacity becomes available, sharply curtailing multi-tasking and increasing overall output.

<u>Distribute work as it arrives</u>
Jobs are immediately handed out to the next person in line, no work is held back. Each person has multiple jobs on his/ her desk, so multi-tasking is rampant.

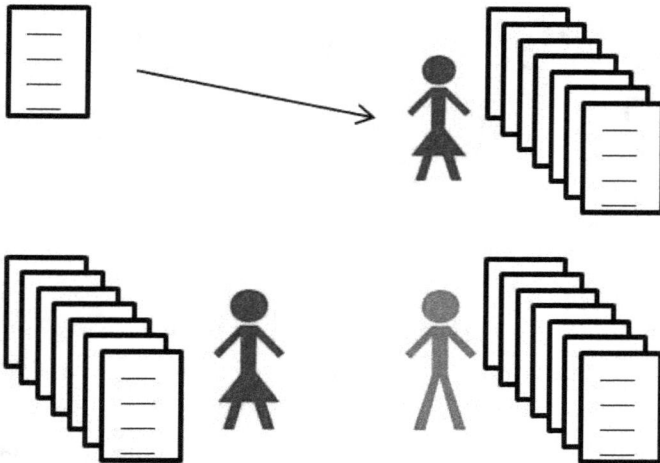

Pool and distribute work as resources are available

Work is kept in a common pool. Each person is allowed a small number of active jobs. Only when a person completes a job, is the next job in the queue released—multi-tasking is greatly reduced.

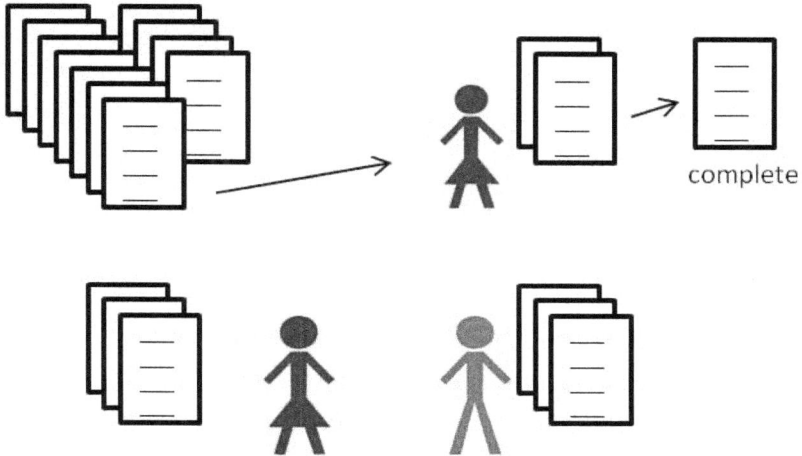

complete

4. Take the opportunity to re-prioritize the pool of work based on the current level of urgency, so the most urgent task is always "next" in the pool.

5. Increase focus by scheduling meetings or times to discuss issues rather than allowing interruptions to happen throughout the day.

6. Institute "quiet time." Make periods of the day interruption free by not allowing meetings, phone calls, or emails to break people's focus on their tasks.

7. Monitor how many things people are working on, especially your most critical folks. Your best people are the ones who typically get pulled in the most directions, so pay special attention they don't get overloaded and can finish tasks before accepting more.

8. Don't be afraid to kill or freeze tasks, projects, initiatives or other work that is less critical. One of the key roles of leadership is to set the priorities and sometimes you need to step in to control the multi-tasking.

Reducing multi-tasking is not about having people do less work, or only do one type of activity. People can wear multiple 'hats,' they just need to complete one task before they move onto the next. They will spend less time re-starting tasks, and more time completing it, so their output increases dramatically. It's not unusual to find your tasks get done in half the time and people are able to produce twice as much work, with no additional effort. Best of all nearly everyone prefers to work this way. Interruptions are killers—that's the main reason people get into the office early, stay late, or work from home, they get much more accomplished during these times.

Profit Booster Tips

- ✓ To get buy in, ask people if they prefer to work a task through to the finish, or to get interrupted and shifted to something else
- ✓ Take steps to block work from entering the work flow. You'd be surprised by how many ways new activities can get started.
- ✓ Be mindful of what requests you make of your people—when the boss asks for something, it often goes to the top of the priority list. Be sure that's what you want. In my work with state governments, I learned any request that came from the Governor's office went immediately to the top of the to-do list—all the time.
- ✓ Take work away from people, don't expect setting priorities alone will reduce multi-tasking

Practice 12:
Relate Everything Back to the Big Picture
⌖➕

When you are at or near the top of the organization the big picture of the whole enterprise is pretty apparent to you, it's part of your every day work. So it is easy to forget not everyone sees the enterprise as you do, from that global picture. In fact because people are focused on their particular role and all it demands they are usually not looking at the bigger picture. In many companies most of the employees do not have a good understanding of the business as a whole nor even of how the work they do connects to the work done in other areas. If people are operating in a way that hurts the flow or the process somewhere else we really shouldn't be too surprised about it. They probably are doing it from a lack of understanding of the bigger picture more than anything else.

There is an old parable from India, I believe, about five blind men describing an elephant which illustrates the problem well. One blind man is holding the trunk of the elephant and says an elephant is like a great python, long and strong. The next one has his arms wrapped around one of the elephant's legs and says, "No an elephant is like a great tree, thick, and immovable." The third blind man is touching a tusk and describes the elephant as like a spear, long and smooth and sharp. The fourth one is touching an ear and says, "No, the elephant is like the leaves of a great palm tree waving in the wind." And the last blind man, holding the tail, disagrees with all the rest and describes the elephant like a rope. They each understand one part of the elephant well, but none of them has any clue what the entire elephant really looks like.

Anything you do to expose people to the larger picture of the business will help them to better align themselves with the goal and the rest of the company. But here are a few simple practices you can try:

1. Explain everything within its larger context. Don't take context for granted, you have it because of your perspective near the top of the business, others most likely don't have the full context. Whether you are talking about a customer issue, engineering concern, financial issue, capital expenditure, production problem or anything else, start it off by pulling back to the a higher level and explaining the context. When people start to understand the "whys" of the larger picture, alignment will improve.

2. Post pictures around the company showing what things look like at different stages of your process and at the customer. Pictures or physical samples of a part's evolution after each step of production show people what happens before and after their step of the process enabling them to appreciate aspects of quality, technical requirements and challenges. It connects them more closely to how everyone works together to get the result. Pictures of how the customer uses your products or services or their production line, help people connect what they do to the needs and expectations of the market.

3. Explain why things need to be done a certain way. When people understand the reasons for a particular design approach, engineering or process decisions it becomes much easier for them to align their efforts to execute it. This is especially important whenever you make a change to something. Always give an explanation of why it is being done. People will adapt to it much faster when they understand the reasons.

4. Connect things to their financial implications. Making money is the goal so everything is and should be evaluated in terms of its financial impact. As a top manager you do this automatically, but much or most of the business does not see or understand these things unless we provide that information. Explaining the larger financial context and rationale of decisions or actions will reduce the tendency of people to see things as arbitrary and enable them to appreciate better how to align their efforts with the company's.

Start providing the context of the big picture today. Better understanding always promotes better teamwork and gets better results.

Profit Booster Tips

- ✓ Assume people don't understand your finances, business model, markets or strategy
- ✓ Take the time to logically connect for people how actions in one area impact others, the customers, and the business as a whole
- ✓ Explain how an action led to a problem somewhere else so people see *why* it needs to be addressed

Practice 13:
Focus on Throughput

There is a natural bias toward managing cost (operating expense) in companies. Cost seems more tangible, we can see and manage what we spend every day. Cost is easily assigned to individual departments and managers so it is perfect for managing and promoting accountability with mechanisms like budgets and other controls. And cost ties directly to the bottom line—every dollar we save should add to our profits. But "saving money" is not why our business exists, and over the long run, we cannot continually increase profits by focusing our attention on reducing operating expense. It's also limited in terms of its impact. Cost can only be cut so far, at some point cuts start to impact revenues, and then they lose their effect altogether.

Throughput, the money our business generates through sales, on the other hand is much more aligned to the goal of <u>making</u> more money. It's why companies exist and increasing Throughput has a much greater impact on the bottom line than a similar percentage reduction in labor. Yes, throughput is messy. Generating money through delivered sales requires the entire organization to accomplish. It's not assignable to a single department and no one function can control it on its own. That's just how it is. It is not simple.

Here are some practices to help you and your organization more effectively focus on increasing your Throughput.

1. Make Throughput the most visible and most frequently discussed metric. You don't have to seek out someone to blame, you don't need to single anyone out (in fact you shouldn't). You just need to talk about it. Very quickly people will start to talk among themselves and figure out better ways to collaborate and accelerate shipments. Below is an example of a simple metric I call the "On-The-Line Chart." It shows people

how the company is doing each day in terms of achieving its deliveries for the period. The line represents the target (cumulative each day of the period). The bars represent the actual shipments made (cumulative each day for the period). The goal is to "get on the line" (or above), and it keeps everyone focused on the goal. It can be easily set up in Excel or any simple report program.

"On-the-line Chart"

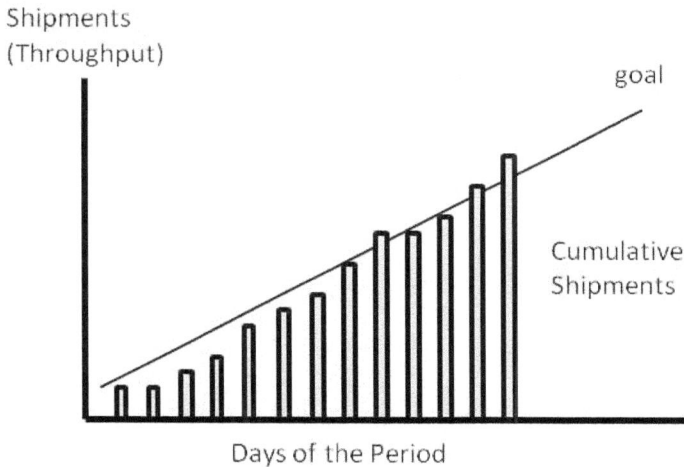

Shipments
(Throughput)

goal

Cumulative
Shipments

Days of the Period

2. Inquire about what limits us from delivering more. There is always something limiting your Throughput. (For more on this see Practice Four: Finding Your Constraints) Getting people thinking about it, looking for it and acting on it is essential to getting it done. So ask about it. When your team understands you care about it, they will too.

3. Ask how any decision or action is going to increase Throughput. So much of most companies' efforts go into cost reduction. People are often not thinking about how to impact Throughput. By asking regularly about the impact on Throughput and

encouraging people to look for solutions to increase Throughput, people will start to shift their focus too.

4. Get out into your operation and look for the bottlenecks. Where is work backing up? Are your people or equipment working on the tasks that result in delivering Throughput? Being busy is not the same thing as producing results. Getting close to your business will improve your ability to know where there are opportunities to increase Throughput, making you much more effective as a leader. (For more on this see the Blue Light practice in this section)

Generating Throughput is the way you drive profits. When you increase your shipments, you lower your cost per unit, make your customers' happy and drive more revenues into the company. So make it the focus of your attention and communication every day. Your team will start to get aligned and work more effectively to produce it.

Profit Booster Tips

- ✓ Focus on generating *flow*, when work backs up Throughput goes down
- ✓ Monitor work-levels or inventory to find what's slowing your Throughput down
- ✓ Don't be fooled by departmental production figures—it's not Throughput until it's shipped to a customer
- ✓ Get departments talking to each other about their challenges and how to address them
- ✓ Reward everyone when Throughput goes up, and engage everyone in finding solutions when it goes down
- ✓ Monitor your Throughput daily. Most companies generate their greatest revenues in the last week of the month, quarter and year. Why can't you do that every day?

Practice 14:
Use Measures to Provide Fast Feedback on Ideas
🕐👍

Generating new ideas, solutions, and changes is critical to the on-going success of every business. Your company must find ways to improve and adapt or you will not progress and may not survive. Not every change or new way of doing things is an 'improvement.' It's essential we have a way to get the right new ideas; the changes needed to take us forward and help us to be more profitable. Making it a practice to devise effective ways to measure the impact of changes is a great way to improve your results, and motivate people to generate more and more new thinking.

Obviously, whenever we introduce a change we do it to make something better. We expect it will lead to helping us make more money. Very often it is difficult to judge the impact of that action immediately. Sometimes it is an improvement in a local area and it's hard to know how it will translate into bottom line results. Worse still, in many cases, the impact of the idea may take a long time, a month or even a year, before you see the results on the financial statements. By that time so many other things have happened and changed that it's virtually impossible to confirm if the new idea was the cause of the results.

Developing an interim measure to judge the impact of a new idea is a great way to clarify and accelerate that process. And when you can find out very quickly if a new idea or change is working, you reduce trial and error and get much better results faster. It also has another important benefit.

The practice is to devise a way to test whether any new idea or change is producing the desired result, right away, without having to wait. Creating a fast feedback loop will enable you to know if something is working and we should continue or spread it, if it needs to be adjusted or tweaked, or if it's a bust and we should stop it. Here are a few guidelines to practice yourself and to guide your team to follow:

1. Clearly define what the idea or change is.
2. List the expected benefits of the new idea or change. Will it help improve product quality? Increase on-time delivery? Reduce work time? etc. Try to be as specific as possible.
3. Define the mechanism by which the change will produce these benefits. This is critical. The mechanism is the pathway or logic by which the change will eventually lead to making more money. Ask yourself, "If the solution is working what will we see happening?"
4. Create a simple measurement to judge if the action is having the desired impact. Choose the measurement that gives you the fastest feedback, even if it's not perfect. Getting an early indication of how your idea is working is far more important than having a perfect indicator. You can always dig deeper to check it further.

In addition to having a way to check and improve your ideas without losing time waiting for the results, I mentioned there is another big benefit. When you have a way to measure quickly the risk of trying new ideas goes down dramatically, and so does people's fear of "making a mistake." As you start to do it you can even turn it into a bit of a game. What new ideas can we come up with this week? How can we tell if they are working and what did we learn from last week's efforts?

Designing these measures is not always easy, and it definitely takes practice. If you get in the habit of trying to find interim measures, and encouraging your people to do it, you will find that you can get pretty good at it quickly. And as you do you will see a marked rise in both the number of new ideas people generate and the quality of those ideas. Being able to launch more effective changes, and to know when they need to be improved upon will enable you to increase performance much faster.

Profit Booster Tips

- ✓ Use this practice on longer or higher investment undertakings in order to catch problems early and make adjustments
- ✓ Require people to come up with intermediate indicators to force them to think through how the solution will produce results
- ✓ Drive analysis based on what the measurement indicates to modify solutions and avoid throwing the baby out with the bath water
- ✓ Make it a weekly game

Chapter 5

Practices for Engagement

"Success means doing the best we can with what we have. Success is the doing not the getting; in the trying not the triumph. Success is a personal standard, reaching for the highest that is within us, becoming all that we can be."   *-Zig Ziglar*

Organizations are first and last, groups of people; groups of people who have come together for a reason, to accomplish a goal. You need people, and you want them to perform at their best. To accomplish that you must have engagement. Unfortunately engagement is sorely lacking in companies today. Gallup's annual survey of employee engagement for 2014 shows: "Less than one-third (31.5%) of U.S. workers were engaged in their jobs in 2014."[1] Fully two-thirds of employees are either "not engaged" or "actively disengaged." Ouch!

The fact this is the lowest (best) figure they have reported since the start of the surveys in 2000, doesn't make me feel any better. What it means for you is there is a huge source of untapped potential that companies are not utilizing well today. And because engagement is so low, there is a huge upside to even a small gain. If your company is at the average point (33%) turning just 1 in 6 of the remaining people would increase the engagement of your workforce by 50%. It's a goldmine of opportunity for growth and profitability.

Far too much attention has been given to 'empowerment' as the key to capitalizing on people's talents. Empowerment falls far short of what produces great teams, and points us in the wrong location to unlock engagement. When companies seek to empower employees, they are primarily talking about what responsibilities they are giving people. Do we really think putting someone "in charge of" something, or giving them the freedom to make a decision is the same as getting them to *care* about it so much they will not rest until they have the best solution? I don't think so.

When we focus on empowerment we leave out the most important part of the equation, the *desire* to do the best. Daniel H. Pink, in his powerful bestseller **Drive: The Surprising Truth About What Motivates Us,**[2] makes a compelling case that intrinsic motivation (that which comes from within us) is by far more powerful than 'extrinsic' motivation, which comes from the outside. Engagement taps into the forces within people, driving their desires and actions. Engagement is empowerment on steroids (in a good way). It is the combination of being empowered, and deeply caring about the outcome. If you had the choice between empowering people and getting them to care about the result, which one would you choose? I know I'd take the caring part every time. When people care about the outcomes and the people around them, they will find a way. When they are empowered, they will simply make a decision.

And engagement is becoming more and more important in business, simply because of the pace of change in the world. Without engagement—the active, thoughtful and energetic participation of people—the only solution for leaders is to be 'prescriptive' everywhere across the company. One can try to script everything out (detailed steps, processes, decision rules, actions and reactions) for the organization—and there is definitely some value in going through that process—but it will never cover every situation or circumstance. In addition to the massive work required to do this, you run the very likely risk of missing things or getting it wrong.

Committing to prescriptive methods also means you are signing up for the process of maintaining and modifying all of those guidelines. With the ever increasing rate of change in business today, this becomes an enormous burden to carry, and you still won't always get it right. Engagement, then, becomes the more attractive and perhaps the only viable path to growing profits consistently over time.

Creating Engagement

As with great teamwork in general, we readily recognize when people are engaged and striving to give their best. Just watch someone's face when they tell you about something important they have done. Their pride is so obvious. When people are engaged they not only accept challenges, they seek them out. Their minds work on issues long after working hours. They struggle and stretch, though no one is there pushing them. They don't always succeed, for sure. Engaged people keep trying and keep thinking because it matters to them. Engagement only happens when people deeply care about what they do.

While you may be able to enforce compliance with rules, you can never get people's best by forcing it out of them. Engagement comes from within a person, when they care so much they give their best. Fortunately, there seems to be something inherent in human beings which craves to become engaged, perform at our best and be an important part of a great team. We want to be challenged, to stretch ourselves, to perform well, to solve a difficult problem. This is particularly true of our professional lives, because we spend so much of our life on the job. No one wants to devote the majority of his life to doing something he doesn't care about. We want to be engaged, we want to feel proud of ourselves, especially at work.

Our job as leaders is to create the environment where this quality can shine. Where people are positioned to succeed, and care enough to put their minds and their hearts into it. No financial bonus plan, employee of the month program, or other "incentives" can create the kind of engagement great teams have. Those things are simply the symbols, the outcomes of engagement, not the reason for it. When you get people engaged, especially when you have good alignment to start, you cannot help but have a successful, profitable and growing company.

The practices below are designed to promote engagement across your company. Engagement means people are involved in a very active way in their work. Engaged people have thrown themselves into their work and care about it, and the results they get. They are eager, questioning, even challenging. They are thinking about solutions and problems. They are "going the extra mile," and spending more time addressing challenges than complaining about them. This is the vision of what people on a great team look like in action. Having a clear simple vision of "what good looks like" is very helpful in keeping us focused on the goal and working towards it. When you know what good looks like you can always compare it to what your company looks like and take action.

Look around your organization and ask yourself what you see. What aspects of engagement do I see? Which ones are lacking or could be improved? If you decide that engagement could be better, keep reading and start practicing something new to foster and support the engagement you want to see.

Practice 15:
Picture What Engagement Looks Like
🕐👍

Now that I gave you a general picture of what engagement looks like in the above introduction, you need to sharpen the picture for your specific business. Picturing what we want to occur, or as I like to say, "what good looks like," is a great way to anchor our mind and focus our efforts. I have discussed several practices in the alignment section already offer terrific ways to move you toward your goals. Starting with a clear picture of what an engaged employee looks like perfect practice for increasing people's engagement in your business. Keep in mind this will look different based on each person's roles and responsibilities. You are likely to be forming multiple pictures based on what your team looks like.

Here are some questions to help you for your own pictures:

1. What would an engaged person do routinely during the day?
2. How would they set priorities?
3. How do they know when something is not right and what would they do about it?
4. When would they ask for help or escalate a problem?
5. What kinds of things would they be doing to improve their area?
6. How would they ensure they are doing a quality job?
7. How would they determine if they had a good day?
8. What things would they NOT be doing?

Creating these simple pictures helps both you and your team members to understand how to contribute more to the success of the business. You can use these pictures as a template and compare it to how your team is operating in reality. The gaps between your picture and what is actually happening give you the key for where to focus your efforts to increase people's engagement.

Profit Booster Tips

- ✓ Use your best performers as a model—what do they do that makes them so successful
- ✓ Ask yourself what you would do if you had that job
- ✓ To have the greatest impact in increasing engagement, focus on the biggest gaps across the whole department or business
- ✓ Take notes on what people are doing today vs. your picture of what good looks like and use them later to evaluate your progress

Practice 16:
Innovate on Process
👍➕

Getting engagement from your team is difficult. Getting productive, effective engagement to increase your profits is even harder. Many of us have experienced the failure of the "suggestion box" approach at some point in our careers. It usually goes something like this........

A company decides it needs more engagement from its team and puts out suggestion boxes to try to tap into the wealth of knowledge and experience of its team by giving them a simple way to provide improvement ideas. Initially, the boxes are filled and management is excited. As we go through the flood of ideas, we discover most of them are not very useful at all. They won't increase sales or reduce costs or win us more customers. They often cost money to implement or require significant time commitments. In short, the lion's share of the suggestions are non-starters that we are not going to pursue.

When the team sees no actions being taken on their ideas, they quickly get disillusioned and the whole process becomes an act of lip-service that will soon be labeled as another "flavor of the month." Trust is damaged, people clam up again and it becomes even harder to gain engagement. Sound familiar?

The underlying reason for this type of failure is people do not have a clear guide for determining which ideas are good for the company and which are not. And on top of it, management does not have an objective way of communicating why an idea should or shouldn't be pursued. It all appears to be an arbitrary process.

On simple solution to this problem and to channel people's knowledge into effective engagement is to use your existing processes as the basis for improvement and innovation. Businesses run on processes. They are essential to developing standard ways of working to ensure quality, consistency and adherence to the standards and values of the company.

Every department has their own policies for everything from completing orders, to requisitioning materials, for handling customer complaints, for product design, setting up equipment and pretty much everything else. The people who work in these processes everyday know them better than anyone. They see all their flaws and shortcomings. So it's the perfect place to focus their efforts.

When you identify the shortcomings in a process, you can modify it and transfer the improvement to the whole company, not just a single person. Now you will have something with real benefit for your company and you can eliminate the source of problems undermining your profits and consuming your time. There are a few key elements that will help you ensure this pays off for you:

1. Clarify why each process exists. Understanding is critical to engagement. If people don't clearly understand the purpose of a process, it is easy for it to get distorted.

2. Use T, I, OE to evaluate the effectiveness of any idea. Good ideas increase profits so they will have a positive impact on T, I, and OE. (See **Practice Six** for more on these measurements.) Ask people to connect their ideas to how it will impact these measures—even if they cannot quantify it fully, the act of doing it will improve their ideas immensely. This also gives you a way to explain why the idea will or won't be implemented so that it is not arbitrary.

3. Don't be afraid to run a test of the change. If it's not obvious the change is a good one, run a test in one area, on a single machine, or for a short period of time to confirm the results.

4. Formalize the change. Once an idea has been proven and approved for inclusion make sure it gets formally written down, incorporated into the process, and communicated to everyone affected.

5. Recognize the contributors. You will get more mileage out of the change and foster a higher degree of engagement if you then make a public recognition of those who made it happen.

Whether it is a small monetary award, some added benefit like an extra vacation day, or simply highlighting the contribution in your newsletter, it's critical to acknowledge the contribution.

6. Processes are a great focal point for innovation, because they capitalize on where people's knowledge and experience is strongest. They provide a way to readily scale ideas and incorporate them you're your operations.

Profit Booster Tips

- ✓ Increase your leverage by picking out processes which are particularly in need of improvement and target them first
- ✓ Be patient as people learn how to connect their ideas to T, I, OE and the purpose of the process. It will take time for people to think in this way.
- ✓ Be open and receptive to the suggestions. As the manager you often have a stake in the existing process, you may even have created it. So modifications may feel like criticisms. Resist this temptation and recognize if your team improves the process, you as the manager will also get credit for it.

Practice 17:
Use Images to Show 'What Good Looks Like' (WGLL)
👍➕

Every business leader will agree on the importance of having a clear company vision. It's essential, and it's also insufficient. It is still difficult for most people in the company to relate the company vision to what they do every day. In order to really engage people in your business you should take the next step and create a clear vision of 'what good looks like' for each group or even the individual level.

By now you can tell I am a big fan of pictures, visuals, and mental images to reflect how things 'should be.' They are extraordinarily effective in increasing performance, especially engagement in a business. It is enormously cumbersome and risky to try to 'prescribe' how people should act and how they should make decisions. Defining 'what good looks like' is the way out of that trap, and also the most effective way to unleash people's knowledge, skills, and their innate desire to do a great job. It is also a great way to radiate best practices and multiply your efforts dramatically.

I strongly suspect you already have a pretty good picture in your head of how a department or function should operate. And if not it shouldn't take you long to articulate it. This practice will help you leverage that knowledge and spark engagement on a new level and it can be used in a number of situations.

1. Instead of trying to create a specific formula for people to follow, write down and capture the desired outcome—"our customers feel valued and appreciated," "we pass on only good parts to the next operation," "we are continually reducing set-up times." Instead of always communicating "how" to do something we are giving people a way to see the outcome, the "what" we want to accomplish. This not only enables you to

connect vision to daily work, but it also engages people in finding better ways to get there. Who knows the details better after all than the people who work a specific job every day? When they focus on outcomes they will find novel, efficient and more effective ways to get there—things you never would have thought of.

2. Add parameters to your descriptions. Giving people some parameters to operate within will sharpen their focus and get them working on the right kind of solutions to get the desired result. You might say: "See if you can find a way to do this without spending more than $100," or "look for solutions that utilize existing resources," or "be sure that your solutions don't make the work harder for downstream operations."

3. Convert your description into a more tangible form. Provide a perfect part as a model (or imperfect ones that show what isn't right), share a recording a great customer service call, provide a chart, checklist, photograph, or drawing showing what good looks like. (There are some real world examples below.)

4. Share your image with your team. Post the image or diagram in a prominent location, or paint lines on a shelf where parts should be so everyone can see at a glance if something is missing. Hang a checklist with pictures of all the needed items to do a machine changeover, or all the documents that need to be in a bid submission.

5. Reinforce the use of the image to guide actions and decisions. Refer to the image or description often and you will quickly get people focused on making it a reality. Instead of saying "you need to go produce more of this part," refer to the empty slots on the painted shelf and remind them we need to keep them full. This will not only get you the parts that are missing right now, but it will teach people how to make the correct decisions themselves in the future.

6. Capitalize on your best people and best practices. Every company has top performers and instances of exceptional performance. Take note of these people and moments and use

them to create examples of "what good looks like." If it could be done once, you can do it every time.

Examples:

- A manufacturer wanted to be sure his bottleneck always had enough of the right parts so it was always producing. He put up an easel and strips of sticky labels on which they had printed customer order information—one label, one order; one strip, one day's scheduled production, with current day's schedule at the left and future days going out to the right. To ensure all the needed items were there to assemble and pack the order, the team was to peel off the label and stick it on the job's paperwork package as soon as all the items were on-hand and ready. If a label was still on the easel something was still missing. WGLL was all of today's labels were gone from the strip—that meant that everything was there to complete today's schedule. Any label still on the board for today's schedule meant that something was missing and something should be done about getting it. Anyone could look at the board and in a glance see how they were doing, and what corrective action was needed.

- Another company used a simple cover sheet attached to every job moving through their engineering department. It contained a checklist with all the items the engineers needed to execute the company's design projects. WGLL was all boxes checked on the sheet. Anyone could quickly look at the sheets and know what was missing and what actions were required.

- The 'Blue Light' image discussed in Practice Five is another great example of a simple powerful image to model.

So get in the practice of creating and using images of 'what good looks like' to communicate what you want to happen. People will put their minds and their attention into making this picture a reality, and your business will run better and better with less and less effort on your part.

Profit Booster Tips

- ✓ Post examples, lists, and pictures of 'what good looks like' (WGLL)
- ✓ Share examples of novel ways your people have found for creating "what good looks like" as a recognition and further model for others to follow
- ✓ Pay attention to individual performance to find high-performers and communicate their methods
- ✓ Get people to compare the images of 'what good looks like' to what's actually happening, so they can self-correct
- ✓ Resist the temptation to 'prescribe' solutions—illustrations of successful methods work far better

Practice 18:
Spark Creative Problem Solving
🕐➕

One of the biggest challenges leaders face with regard to engagement is how to get people to be creative in solving problems. It's a sure sign engagement is lacking when the answer to every problem is to hire more people or otherwise, "throw money at it." We know as leaders there are always creative, often simple ways to solve even the most difficult problems. But there is no way we can dive into everything to find such answers. We need our people to look deeper, tap their imaginations, exercise their brains, and find innovative ways to get things done.

A few years ago I was exposed to a great practice for doing this in the book, **The Three Laws of Performance: Rewriting the Future of Your Organization and Your Life** by Steve Zaffon and Dave Logan. It's a terrific read and I highly recommend it. This practice is derived directly from their concepts. The three laws they articulate are:

1. How people perform correlates to how situations occur to them
2. How a situation occurs to them arises in language
3. Future-based language transforms how situations occur to people (descriptive language binds us.)

The first law addresses how we address any situation--how we perform, depends on how we perceive the situation. In other words, our perception of something is the reality of it to each of us. The second law highlights language as the currency of our perception. It is through words that something makes sense or exists for us. And by understanding and being sensitive to the words being used, we can understand how a situation occurs to someone.

Take a simple example—a potential customer decided to give his business to someone else—that's the fact of the situation. But the perception, how it occurs to different people, can vary widely:

> *"I knew our prices were too high, all that customer cares about is price."*
> *"What a relief, that account was going to take so much of my time for almost no revenue."*

There are many ways any situation can occur to people and the language we choose to use shapes and expresses it.

This is where the third law comes in and is so powerful. The second part of it—descriptive language binds us—illustrates the language we use frames and limits how we look at any situation, and thus limits how we look at solutions. If the salesperson "knows" his price is the problem, how likely will he be to look for other reasons for the missed sale or to try different solutions? Probably not very likely at all. He has already determined what the problem is and bracketed the space for the solution—lower prices.

This happens in all kinds of situations. I had a client where every time a machine broke down, the discussion turned to how old their equipment was. The effect was devastating, it was the equivalent of saying "oh well, there is nothing we can do." It didn't matter that later the cause turned out to be a bolt wasn't tightened properly by a new operator. Descriptive language like this may seem harmless, but in reality its repeated use kills any form of creative problem solving.

The way to break out of this self-limiting behavior is to use "future-based language," to create a different future for the situation. The salesperson who knew his prices were too high might be coached to investigate how his product or service offered greater value to the next customer and reduced other costs, making it a bargain compared to the competition. In the case of the company with the old machines one might ask what steps should be taken to prevent breakdowns the next time? In both cases a simple change to future-based language opens up a realm of new possibilities that had been shut out by the descriptive language people were using to define the situation.

Here is a simple practice to help you spark more creative problem solving and prevent people from falling into the trap of seeing things only one way.

1. Listen to how people describe or characterize situations. Listen in particular for emotionally-charged language. This will help you to understand how a situation occurs to people. You will be surprised by how quickly you can identify people's perception and how easily you can see the limitations they put on themselves.

2. Avoid the analysis trap. We all have a tendency to want to understand why something happened, to have an explanation for it. But in reality analysis is only valuable in helping us to take better actions the next time. When the conversation turns to explaining why something happened it almost always ends up in people defending and hardening their positions—the opposite of what you want.

3. Re-shape the conversation using future-based language. Talk about next time, ask people to design ways to prevent the situation occurring the same way again, guide them to tell you all that is necessary to make it go better in the future. This kind of discussion taps into the creative side of people's brains and liberates them from the limitations of their perception.

4. Try this phrase if you find the solutions always seem to involve a lot of time and money: "What can we do about it today?" Often we view larger problems as requiring big, long-term fixes, which don't usually happen fast. Ask this question a couple of times and nudge people to think about immediate actions, without waiting for a committee to be formed, an investigation to be done or some other distant activity.

Getting past the limitations people set on themselves is not easy, and leaning on the Three Laws of Performance is an effective practice to help you.

Profit Booster Tips

- ✓ Listen seeking to really understand how a situation occurs to people
- ✓ Recognize how someone perceives a situation will shape how they perform in that situation
- ✓ Check yourself and avoid the trap of describing the situation more and more, you are just digging the hole deeper
- ✓ Focus on the future and use language to re-shape how people approach the situation
- ✓ Use "what can we do about it today?" as a regular prompt to drive short term action

Practice 19:
Catch People Doing Something Right
👍➕

We all do better with a little praise. And being mindful of the balance you strike between praise and critique is a great way to promote the right actions and increase engagement.

As leaders we are often prone to look for and see the flaws in things because that's what we need to fix to get better. This is not a bad thing at all. Sometimes much of the discussion in companies can be often around what went wrong, why it didn't get done, what we are doing about it, etc. When finding flaws is the pre-dominant practice, it can quickly lead to disengagement. Conversations can descend into blaming, covering your backside, and generally make people gun-shy about taking actions or being decisive. Remember the statement, "tell me how you measure me and I will tell you how I am going to behave." Whatever you reinforce with your praise or criticism is what you will get. You want your team to engage in more and more of the *right* actions to drive your business ahead. So finding daily opportunities to catch people doing something good is a great way to promote and reinforce those positive steps. There's nothing wrong with finding flaws and pointing out things we need to do better, that's part of management and of improving any team. Just make sure you monitor yourself and the reactions you are getting so you keep a good balance between praise and critique. Here are some suggestions to practice this concept:

- When you call out bad behavior, make it a practice to point out at least two examples of good behavior
- Instead of speaking directly about the behavior you didn't want, express it as what you DO want. "It's really important we get all functions to attend these meetings because everyone's input is critical. We want to produce the best product for our customers so we can't afford to miss something important."

- Resist the temptation to drag out past failures or shortcomings. We cannot change the past so telling people things like: "I don't want this to go like last time when we…" really doesn't help much. It only communicates people should avoid mistakes, instead of producing solutions.
- When you do feel you need to address bad behavior, try this old technique I learned coaching youth sports. Start by pointing out something good that was done and then proceed to highlight that area or behavior needing improvement. "I like the way you made that pass. Do you think you can make it even quicker the next time?"
- Or maybe this one: If you see something you think needs to be improved in that area, ask about it. "By the way, I have noticed sometimes ____ is happening. What do you think we could do about that?" You can suggest they think about it and you'll drop by in a day or two and see what they have to say. Now they are aware of the problem, don't feel criticized and are focused on fixing it—a trifecta!

There's nothing wrong with highlighting when people are doing something wrong or contrary to policy or procedure. Just keep in mind the old adage that Dale Carnegie was so fond of: "You attract a lot more flies with honey than with vinegar." This practice costs nothing and is a great way to promote engagement in your team.

Profit Booster Tips

- ✓ Start with a positive before going to your criticism
- ✓ Make a mental list of some of the things the person has done right, this will keep your comments more in balance
- ✓ Always explain the impact on the company when you do make a criticism so your comment does not seem arbitrary or like nit-picking

✓ Remember the "right" behavior or decision is your objective, not blaming
✓ Pay attention to the climate in the company, are people risk averse? Or more inclined to be pro-active or to innovate? Adjust your tactics accordingly.

Practice 20:
Share your Ideas Last
🕐➕

Most leaders already understand when the boss shares his ideas first you have virtually eliminated the chance of getting any different ideas. Creating engagement and bringing out the best in your people requires them to learn to think and act on their own. If people are not accustomed to solving problems and making decisions on their own, it's critical you help them develop the ability and confidence to act effectively on their own. It's easy to jump and propose or prescribe a solution when there is an issue needing to be addressed. The more you as a leader take on the role of problem-solver, the more people will depend on you to play that role and the less they will exercise their minds and think an issue through. What's worse still is when you are proposing the solution—it's yours and not theirs. They have no ownership of it, so they are less likely to work through any kinks in the idea. And if the solution fails, there is no responsibility—it was your "bad solution" after all.

So whenever you are discussing a problem or situation with your team—fight the urge to present a solution, ask them to come with their ideas first. Force your team to consider the issue and develop solutions. If nothing is immediately forthcoming, give them a short, fixed amount of time to come back with their ideas—like an hour. Let's face it, thinking through most issues does not take week, or even a day usually. When we ask someone to come back with a plan in a week, they will usually wait until the deadline is near and work the appropriate amount of time on it. Why lose all that time? Why not say, "Okay folks, I'm going to step out for 20 minutes, talk about it, and let's hear your ideas when I return."

This will force people to think for themselves and consider different sides of an issue. You can always offer your own ideas after you hear theirs if you are concerned about the direction of things. And in any event they will have taken a critical step in getting more and more engaged in the business and its success.

Profit Booster Tips

- ✓ If the group's idea is "good enough," let it be and keep your idea to yourself so they retain full ownership
- ✓ If you are having trouble not blurting out your solution, write it down on a piece of paper and keep it to yourself to reduce the urge
- ✓ Try combining this practice with the next one to increase engagement and make sure that the solutions provide the best bottom line impact

Practice 21:
Provide Opportunities for Growth
➕

Did you know surveys show the number one reason employees leave a company is "Lack of opportunities for advancement"[3]? A survey of 2012 college graduates found exactly the same thing at the top of the list, so your newest team members are looking for exactly the same thing.[4] People want to grow, they want to have a future offering them new challenges, increased responsibility, and increased earnings potential. In other words, your people are already fertile ground for growing engagement. At the same time companies routinely talk about both the lack of flexibility they have in their workforce and the cost and challenges in hiring.

There is a great opportunity for a win-win here. Cross training is an excellent and easy way to increase your flexibility and also provide a simple growth opportunity for your team. If you have someone good at running a machine, find time to get them on a new machine so they can grow their skills, and give you back-up capacity to offset the challenges of absenteeism and vacations. Or give them some added responsibilities. If they have only been working in accounts payable, give them some past due receivables and let them try their hand at collecting them.

Rather than providing a list of all the things you can do to provide growth opportunities, many of which require substantial investments of time or money, here are some other simple things you can do to increase growth opportunities with little or no investment.

1. Self-training: provide employees with manuals, SOP's, company training materials or books to help people develop themselves and increase their skills, even on their own time

2. Use people in a support role to management or other departments. More often than not your skilled people are doing

a host of tasks that do not require their full skill. Offloading these tasks (especially if the area is a bottleneck or has a backlog of work) will free up your skilled resources to get more work done. It will also expose the support person to new jobs and let them observe and acquire new skills by observation. These people are great candidates for filling vacancies there in the future. Asking for volunteers with these roles is a great way to make growth opportunities available to all—and don't forget to explain it this way when you ask.

3. Include them in existing meetings and discussions. Adding a junior person to a meeting with higher level managers exposes them to the issues, reports and discussion items they will need to master to get to the next level. You can do it without any additional effort.

4. Get them to develop a career growth path and discuss with them simple ways they can grow and prepare themselves. Ask them to identify the skills they need and come with strategies to acquire them. You will be surprised at how innovative they will be and how much they will agree to take on themselves.

5. Incentivize them to learn more. You will create more engagement from people if they have a stake in the process. Provide opportunities for people to learn or acquire new skills if they want to come in early or stay late, or to make time by completing their work faster. Then set them up to learn a new skill or pair them with a more senior person or someone in another department.

Providing growth opportunities is an important aspect to promoting engagement. The more people feel the company cares about them and is providing them the opportunities to grow, the more engaged they will be and the less likely to want to move on. Of course you can follow a host of best-practices for employee development, and there are many great resources out there I would encourage you to investigate if you are so inclined. Trying these simple, low-effort activities will enable you to better address this need. In the process you will undoubtedly see who is most hungry and motivated to grow. If you do decide to invest more time or money, you will already know where to focus.

Profit Booster Tips

- ✓ Don't feel you have to have all the answers or provide a formal process for growth, most people will already have their own ideas and be willing to invest their time in it
- ✓ Work within existing resources and activities. Lean on things you already have and provide people access
- ✓ Use the company's needs to focus growth opportunities, so people learn the work you need most to be more profitable

Practice 22:
Use Questions
◐ ⊚

Leaders are frequently in a position of having to review other people's ideas. And let's face it, many of the ideas people put forward can be quite weak. How you respond to a less-than-perfect plan or idea can have a big effect on people's level of engagement. Often what sounds like a bad idea is really a good idea communicated in a poor way. You never want to proceed with a bad idea, and if you kill the idea you are very likely to inhibit people from bringing ideas forward in the future, especially if it's done in a public forum.

We don't want to miss out on these ideas by squelching them, before we really understand what it is and why it might work. It's also important to keep in mind people are not always very good at presenting an idea in the first place. Even more frequently people will come with undeveloped ideas, containing flaws or side-effects creating concern. The kernel of the idea may actually be very good, it's just not fully developed or properly tuned to be successful. We all know the expression: "Don't throw the baby out with the bathwater." If we kill people's ideas we not only curtail their motivation to bring ideas forward, we will definitely miss out on good ideas that just needs a little more work to get there.

 A better way to address what looks like a bad idea is through questions. It starts by first understanding what type of a concern or fear you have with someone's suggestion. Usually our concerns will fall into one of three different categories:

- We don't think the idea will solve the problem
- We don't think the solution is cost or time effective
- We are afraid the idea will cause some negative side-effects

First decide which of these issues best reflects your concerns (naturally, you may have concerns that relate to more than one of the categories for any idea). Then formulate a question to put your concern on the table and ask the person if they have thought about it and how they plan to address it. Don't try to solve the problem yourself—it's their idea and if it has merit they will figure out how to address your concern by modifying or adding to their idea. If you try to solve it for them, you take responsibility for its success and you take on the work to make the idea a good one.

Let's say someone is proposing the company purchase a new piece of equipment to increase production capacity and help improve on-time delivery of customer orders. You're concerns might fall into any of the three categories. You might be worried having the new machine won't impact on-time delivery (you don't think the idea will solve the problem). The company is already holding large stocks of finished products—they are just not the right items—so more capacity will not ensure having the right items for customers. In such a case you might say: "We already produce more goods than we can sell with our current capacity. Explain to me how increasing capacity will get us more of the right items?"

Alternatively, you may feel the idea would solve the problem, but you are concerned it is not time or cost effective. So a good question might be: "I understand we are not keeping up with our orders, but don't those machines take 6-9 months to get? We need to come up with a solution addressing this problem right away." Or your concerns might fall into the last category—you are afraid that while the idea would solve the problem, it has too many negative side-effects. I call this the arsenic solution, referring to the long-ago practice of treating certain diseases with arsenic. It was great at killing the disease, but often killed the patient too. In such a case you might ask: "I understand why you want that new machine, but I am worried it will require us to significantly upgrade our waste water system to stay within environmental regulations. Have you thought of that?"

So many good things happen when you shift from striking down ideas to addressing them in this way.

- You reinforce innovation and idea generation
- You prompt better thinking
- You allow ideas to become really good ideas
- You remove the perception that decisions are arbitrary by exposing your reasoning to people
- The company pursues fewer bad ideas
- You build trust
- You don't get stuck spending your time solving people's problems for them

Profit Booster Tips

- ✓ Point people back to T, I, OE to help them connect their idea to the bottom line
- ✓ There is always a question that will expose your concerns, don't speak until you have formed it
- ✓ Keep the big picture in mind, if you solve the problem, you will very likely have to solve the next one yourself too

Practice 23:
Stop the B-Game
🕐➕

Blaming is one of the most destructive forces in a business. We all know how to play the B-game. We simply have to explain why it wasn't our fault, and point the finger in another direction...*any* other direction. Companies that find themselves playing the B-game waste a tremendous amount of time and energy on things that can't be changed and are of no value in getting to a solution. It doesn't take long when the blaming begins to see things falling apart. People stop listening to each other, grudges are formed, and collaboration and engagement are totally shattered.

To keep your team engaged and working together leaders need to stop the B-game in its tracks. This should start with the leadership team setting the example. The first step is for management to recognize two fundamental truths in businesses:

- Problems almost never stem from a single source or a single person
- Most problems are driven by the system, and not by people

In my experience of nearly 30 years in organizations of all sizes across a wide-array of industries, I have rarely come across bad people who willfully tried to hurt their company. It does happen to be sure, but this only applies to a tiny fraction of the issues companies encounter. One finds reasons stemming from a host of factors almost never driven by any single person. And in any event engaging in the B-game is not only a huge drain on the company, it's ultimately a fruitless activity.

When the B-game starts people will do whatever they need to to protect themselves. It's more likely the real issues will be buried or shifted elsewhere. In the end you don't usually get any closer to a solution, and you will certainly damage teamwork, trust and engagement. The key is to ensure efforts are focused on making things better, not on seeking scapegoats. There's a great piece of wisdom a colleague of mine has used for years. It goes like this:

"A job not done, plus reasonable reasons, equals a job not done."

Here are some ways to block the B-game from starting and stop it in its tracks when it rears up in your company.

1. When discussion of a problem begins, express your awareness that the problem was not caused intentionally by any person doing the wrong things. Let everyone know what we are after is a solution, not a scapegoat.

2. Monitor your own words and eliminate any language from your speech construing a problem as coming from "somebody" or some group. Phrases like: "Who was responsible..." "Which department..." "Why didn't you..." "How could this happen..." all signal that we are looking for someone to blame, even if that is not your intent.

3. Shift all the attention to the present and future. "What can we do to fix this?," "How do we prevent this from happening again?," "What is our recovery plan?"

4. Point the solution to processes not people. If the success of your business depends on a person making a complex determination without a clear process or robust set of rules, you will always be at risk of the problem happening over and over. You need to take this as a cue to upgrade your processes.

5. Treat problems as wonderful opportunities to strengthen your process. In the Japanese production system at the core of Toyota's rise to global leadership, problems were viewed as "jewels" because they provided the avenue for improving their processes.

6. Express your total ambivalence about where the problem came from. "I really don't care where the problem came from, we just need to solve it and make sure it doesn't happen again."

7. Take responsibility on yourself. "This thing probably happened because of something I said or didn't say, so let's not waste time on the past, let's get it fixed."
8. Be persistent and consistent with these messages. Don't be afraid to remind people of the reason you are there—to solve the problem.
9. Speak to people one-on-one. If one of your team members is having trouble avoiding the B-game, take them aside and let them know it's not the way your company works. Appreciate their efforts and concerns about the problem, but make it clear how they should be addressing it.

Companies where the B-game is a regular part of daily operations lose an enormous amount of productivity. If this is happening in your business, stopping the practice will lead to immediate improvements in engagement and productivity.

Profit Booster Tips

- ✓ Tune your radar to pick up signs the B-game is being played
- ✓ Establish and enforce the ground rules
- ✓ Point everyone back to the on-going damage of *not solving* the problem
- ✓ Use a joke to diffuse a tense situation—"I'm pretty sure this is all just a government conspiracy anyway, so let's get back to solutions!"

Practice 24:
Rebuild Trust with Appreciations
👍➕

Sometimes teamwork is particularly lacking or relationships between people in the company are strained. Engagement, with the energy, passion and caring that we described above, seems at best a remote possibility. In these cases in particular, rebuilding trust with appreciations is very useful in breaking down the barriers and building a solid platform for engagement.

A sense of feeling appreciated for our efforts is one of the most basic human needs. Saying "thank you" is a custom in every society, illustrating how universal and basic appreciation is to people. One doesn't have to go further than to think how we feel when we don't receive a thank you for even a simple act, to understand how important appreciation is. And when the bonds between people are strained, it becomes, even more important, and even more effective because its absence has been so noticeable.

Whether relations are strained or not, this practice will help you to create a foundation for deep engagement. Like most of these practices, it's neither difficult nor earth shattering, but its highly effective. It works like this.

- Start every staff meeting you run by going around the table and asking each person to appreciate somebody else at the table for something they have done. The only rule is the person must be present and you must tell the group what they did that you are appreciating.
- Everyone must appreciate at least one person, and there is no criteria for determining who or what to appreciate

The process takes very little time and has enormous impact on the dynamics of the meeting. Everyone gains a better appreciation of the contributions each person makes. By requiring everyone to appreciate another we invite people to look for the good. People are better able to see that their colleagues are in fact on the same team and striving toward a common goal. And being appreciated by our colleagues binds us more to them and the common mission we all share. The practice can be repeated at all levels of the organization, and staff meetings are the perfect place to start them.

Profit Booster Tips

- ✓ Appreciate efforts that go "above and beyond" routine expectations
- ✓ Never give insincere praise or appreciation, people can smell it like rotting fish
- ✓ Observe that without any suggestion everyone will have been appreciated by someone after just a few meetings
- ✓ Pay attention to the appreciations others give to learn what your team members value and how they respond to praise from their colleagues
- ✓ Notice how after a few meetings the tone and quality of interaction is improving

Practice 25:
Get Out and Walk Around Every Day
⊕

Make it a practice to wander around your business every single day. Management by walking around has been a term and an approach many successful managers have employed for years. General George McClelland, who commanded Lincoln's Army of the Potomac in the U.S. Civil War, was beloved by his men. He wasn't always the most effective strategist and probably missed more than one opportunity to end the war due to indecision, but he knew how to create engagement. McClelland made it a point to get out among his troops, see how they were doing and make sure that they were as comfortable and well provided for as he could. And that created a powerful fighting spirit, which kept him in his command in spite of his shortcomings.

It doesn't have to take long, and so many good things happen when you do it:

- You see things you wouldn't otherwise—opportunities, problems, complicating factors, extra efforts, etc.
- People see you and feel more connected to you and the business
- Conversations happen that otherwise wouldn't have, so you get a better sense of where your people are, and have the opportunity to communicate important messages to them
- You get a better perspective on your business
- You get a little exercise!

As you walk around make it a point to stop and talk with a couple of different people each day. These are great opportunities to show appreciation, and create a sense of shared purpose. When you engage with your team, you prompt engagement in them. When you provide the example you care about them, who they are, what they are doing, the challenges they face, they will be much more likely to want to engage with you, the business, and the rest of the team. You will learn a tremendous amount about your business in the process, and you will increase the engagement of your team.

Profit Booster Tips

- ✓ Combine this with other practices like the "Blue Light," or "Catch people doing something good"
- ✓ Follow up with people on any issues discussed as soon as you can
- ✓ Look for opportunities to help people and take them, no matter how small
- ✓ Bring observations of both problems and excellent performance to the attention of your staff

Practice 26:
Follow Through Quickly
🕐➕

Nothing stamps out engagement like failure to follow through. When leaders say they are going to do something and then don't it sends clear signals to the team—you're not important, accountability doesn't matter, I'm not a man of action, etc. Talk is cheap, and lip-service is the worst kind of service. So follow the mantra of my grandparents' generation, "Do what you say you are going to do."

There are a couple of tips you can use to improve your ability in this regard. It's easy to get caught up in other things or distracted and forget. It's even easier to find yourself biting off more than you can chew, so try these things to improve your follow through.

- Don't commit to actions you really can't fulfill

- Do the easy stuff right away. If there's an action that can be done quickly do it immediately, no matter how small, it will demonstrate your commitment and strengthen people's belief that they are on a team that cares about each other and the mission.

- Keep a list. Always have a small notebook, or piece of paper and pen or use your smart phone to type a reminder or send yourself an email to prompt yourself

- Be clear about what you commit to- Make sure you tell people exactly what the follow up will be so they have the right expectations. Saying you will look into something is not the same as saying you will fix it, so be clear.

- If you are going to delegate the action, set a clear expectation about when it needs to be done and follow up with the person you assign it to. Follow up also with the party you committed to, to be sure it has happened. You don't need to do everything yourself, but showing you care that it happens communicates volumes.

- Clear your list every day before you go home. Even if you can't complete an action you took on, take some step with it and be sure to communicate it to people. Getting in the practice of doing this before you leave for the evening is a great habit, and it will send you home with a clear conscience and a sense of accomplishment.

Problems happen, how you resolve them is what matters. A restaurant that 'comps' a meal served cold usually gains a loyal customer who will promote the business to all his friends. One that doesn't, buys a critic who will tell everyone to stay away. So take care of the small things and they won't become big things. It's cheap, easy, and so profitable.

Profit Booster Tips

- ✓ Ask people to come to you in the future if they are not getting what they need to do their job—this will further increase their engagement
- ✓ Instruct your managers to do the same so that no one is complaining about the company for lack of the basics

Practice 27:
Become the Obstacle Breaker

Servant Leadership, the approach to management developed by Robert K. Greenleaf, is a very powerful and effective model for promoting engagement in an organization. The principles can actually be found as far back in time as ancient China in the work of Lao-Tzu. One of the core principles is that of the leader serving his team in order to ensure that their most important needs are met. A great way to apply this and foster a higher level of engagement is to become an obstacle breaker for your team.

Removing or helping to overcome the obstacles blocking people from doing their best work clears the way for both better outcomes and better engagement. We all get stuck from time to time and can't seem to move forward due to some obstacle. Sometimes these obstacles will even seem trivial—the software requires me to go into three different screens to update information, the bolts on the machine are old and worn, I always have to go searching for the right tools to do the set-up. If they disrupt people and hold them back from doing a better job, our results will suffer and it will reduce people's level of engagement.

Breaking obstacles for people, no matter how small they are to you, is a clear signal that you are about actions, and not lip-service. When you show you are serious about fixing the issues that keep your people from being more successful and productive, you will immediately increase their engagement. Anyone who is familiar with Servant Leadership is well-acquainted with this practice. When you flip the tables on people by showing them that you care about their success, they will absolutely care more about yours and the company's. And by removing their obstacle you will increase their effectiveness and strengthen the business.

Profit Booster Tips

- ✓ Seek out obstacles—ask people what they wish was different, if there is anything they need, anything making their job harder
- ✓ Ask them to tell you how removing the obstacle would help them and the company
- ✓ If the request is larger than you feel comfortable doing, find something smaller, that can be done quickly and inexpensively to help the situation
- ✓ After you have done something, follow-up to be sure it was successful—and don't be afraid to ask the person for their assistance with something, this is a perfect time for such a request

Practice 28:
Use Financial Incentives Very Carefully
➕

The idea of paying for performance or creating financial incentives is very alluring and a common practice in many industries and roles like sales. At first blush it seems a no-brainer, pay people based on how well they perform and they will perform better. Aside from the challenges of creating individual performance metrics that always align with the company goal, which are massive, there are a number of very real problems stemming from the use of financial incentives and rewards in a company. Understanding these will help you avoid some pitfalls and better shape financial rewards if you do choose to use them.

As soon as you put in place a financially driven pay for performance system, you become married to it. Offering increased pay for increased production may get you a relatively quick jump. What happens when you try to get even more from people? They will expect to be paid for it, even when something like new technology or a very effective advertising campaign serves to make it much easier to perform at a higher level. As soon as you start to tie financial incentives to performance you will have to use these incentives all the time.

Another problem arises when we tie bonuses and payouts to some local performance metric, or even if they are tied to company profits. Everyone will have his or her own perception of what they contributed relative to others. Inevitably some people will receive higher rewards than other people think they deserve, while some will receive less than they think they deserve. There is simply no way to assure everyone's reward will match all the perceptions of what they think is deserved. As soon as this starts people will become de-motivated. Both alignment and engagement will be undermined. So while you may find an initial jump in performance as people strive to increase their earnings, it will almost inevitably turn sour on you and create the opposite effect.

At the same time, a company that succeeds and doesn't share at least some of its success with the employees is inviting resentment and disengagement. So what are you to do?

Over the past 25 years the most effective approaches I have seen have been simple, objective and not based on individual assessments of what is "deserved." If you want to share profits with your team, and I encourage it, use a simple, objective system like sharing a fixed percentage of the profits based on salary. It doesn't try to make personal value judgments about who contributed more, so it won't create the resentments I discussed above. It isn't perfect, but people will understand it and not quibble about who got more than they did.

If you want to reward those who you think did an exceptional job, give them a promotion or a raise for being a top-performer. Remember the importance of career growth and opportunity I discussed earlier. By promoting people you increase their engagement and sense of value and you don't get into the nonsense of everyone debating how much more they should have gotten. It will help you avoid the trap of making money the primary incentive you use to drive your performance.

Profit Booster Tips

- ✓ Don't try to create individual pay for performance plans, they almost never work out in the long run
- ✓ Share profits using a simple formula everyone can understand and relate to
- ✓ Share the fruits of success
- ✓ Keep in mind that financial motivation is not the only or even primary motivator of your people

Practice 29:
Expect the Best from People
👍➕

The title of this practice has a double meaning. First, you want to expect people will do a great job, and you want to convey that confidence you have in them. Second, you want to hold people to high standards, to guide them to stretch to something exceptional, not something adequate.

I don't believe there are very many people whose goal is to do a poor or mediocre job. We spend so much of our lives at work, and so it is important to all of us to get a significant measure of satisfaction from it. We all want to be recognized as doing a great job, performing a critical role, providing an important contribution. What great leaders do is to seed and care for this fertile soil so it produces great results. One important and simple step we can do is to tap into this energy and channel it to get better and better results from our team.

Whenever someone is given a job or project or action to do, we can either be confident they will succeed, or not so confident. It doesn't matter what you feel inside—high confidence or serious doubt—always demonstrate you are confident the person or team will succeed. It costs you nothing to do this, and there is no risk. Expressing confidence will have a profound effect on people and the organization as a whole.

When people hear you are confident in them it sets up the mindset and expectation they will succeed. Confidence is a wonderful thing and people always work better when they feel good about themselves. Studies also show people work harder when they are seeking to live up to expectations, rather than trying to avoid living down to low expectations. It also communicates a positive opinion of the people or team to the rest of the organization so they will trust and support the group better.

Of course you may have very significant concerns about whether a team or person will succeed, don't ignore these. But rather than expressing them as doubts or fears turn them around and use them as guidelines and motivators. So when you express your confidence in a team's ability to solve a problem, include your concerns as positives or strengths you appreciate in the team. If your concern is your team will reach a snap judgment on the problem and hurry out a half-baked solution, your mind might be screaming at you to say: "You guys better analyze this carefully and not launch something that blows up on us like you did the last time." Sure, such a statement gets your concerns out there, but it doesn't communicate confidence or create engagement.

Instead try saying something like: "I have every confidence you will succeed in this because I know you will carefully analyze the data to get to the root problem. I know before launching any solution you will check it thoroughly with others to be sure it doesn't cause problems for other departments." I like phrases like "I know you will..." or "I am looking forward to the..." to fully convey my confidence in someone. Whereas phrases like "I hope you look at..." or "Please be sure to..." convey more concern, worry or mis-trust.

To get people to really reach to go beyond a "satisfactory" solution there are some very simple and effective things you can do:

- Challenge people to do even better than the last time
- Ask them if they think they can beat their previous record, or how they would improve the solution the next time
- Set high expectations and criteria for success
- Ask them how fast something could be done if everything fell into place—then get them to tell you what is needed to make that happen
- Get them to find solutions that cost no money—then be pleased if they find a way to do it for less than you expected

- Share positive customer comments and then feedback that highlights shortcomings to expose opportunities for improvement
- Never use 'optimum,' 'perfect,' 'ideal' or other words which convey something cannot be done better
- Avoid fixed targets and other caps signaling there is a 'maximum' performance—always stay focused on "better than before"

Profit Booster Tips

✓ Look outside your industry or market for examples where people have done similar things much better than your company or industry does them

✓ Focus your thinking on improvements to increase your bottom line and set expectations around those factors

✓ Be impressed with every improvement, but never satisfied

✓ Use successes in one area to motivate others to do better

Chapter 6

An On-Going Practice

"There is no glory in practice, but without practice there is no glory"
  —Unknown

I am quite fond of this quote. On the one hand it reminds us of the critical role of practice, the preparation needed to make success possible. Practice is essential to developing effective teamwork, just as it is to almost everything else we will do in our lives. What I like even more is the way these words remind us that practice is NOT the goal. The glory is elsewhere, there is a larger purpose to what we are doing when we practice.

This reminder is critically important when it comes to Teamwork, in business. Teamwork is not the goal, teamwork is the practice. The purpose of your business is what should drive all of your efforts. Athletic teams don't strive to achieve the best teamwork, they pursue victories and championships. Better teamwork is a 'means' to that end, and it is exactly the same in your business.

Better teamwork is only 'better' when it produces better results. Focusing on the characteristics of great teams: communication, shared values, collaboration, and conflict resolution (to name just a few), can obscure our ability to see the goal or even become 'ends' unto themselves. Should teamwork be measured by something like how well we communicate? How many people can recite and practice the company's shared values?

The only real measure of the quality of our teamwork is the company's financial performance. How well you keep the purpose of your practices in mind will be a major factor in the results you get. Do whatever you can to connect the practices you undertake, indeed all of your actions, to your company's goal.

By identifying whether you have an **alignment** issue or an **engagement** need you can select and apply the practice that will most improve your performance. And that's the key, the more targeted you are the greater the results you will see. The symphony conductor will not devote the majority of the rehearsal to passages the orchestra already plays well. The biggest gains are to come from improving the areas of weakness.

The Importance of Focus

I have a friend who is a golf professional who excels at teaching the game. This is very important in my case because my golf swing needs a lot of help. If you went down a checklist of all of the correct elements of a great golf swing, there would be a multitude of red X's on my swing. My friend's ability to quickly zero in on 1 or 2 key things is what makes him so effective as a teacher. He doesn't spend his time telling me all the things I could change, he shows me the ones that will give me the biggest gains.

This degree of focus is equally important in using teamwork to grow your profits. Fortunately, however you understand your business better than I understand a golf swing. Using that understanding to identify the parts of your organization where there is more leverage for gains than others will help you see results much faster. Imagine applying <u>Alignment Practice Ten: Use Pareto to Stop Wasting Efforts on Trivial Things</u> and you can think of many places where this is needed. You will probably have a greater impact applying it on a bottleneck resource than in a less critical department. We all have limited time and resources to spend, use it where you will derive the greatest returns and don't sweat the rest right now.

This is easily said and not so easily done, of course. The hardest part of achieving a sharp focus is not so much knowing what "to do," but rather what "to stop doing." We are constantly barraged by countless things vying for attention, many of them seemingly urgent or critical. It helps if you keep focused on the goal of your business and your people. Choosing the things that take your business the furthest forward will help you separate the truly important things from the rest.

Building better teamwork—the kind of teamwork that really improves your bottom line—takes work, hard work. And it's an on-going activity. The reality of your business is always changing, evolving, shifting. The dynamics of your team and what is needed to produce results is not a static thing. Competition changes, rules change, customer needs change, distribution channels change, even the members of your team are always changing as people retire or move on and new people join.

Creating alignment and fostering engagement is not something that gets "completed," put in a box, and checked off the list. Teamwork requires regular care and feeding, because it is readily impacted by even routine changes in your business environment.

> *The Sales metrics you put in place two years ago to promote alignment with Operations, may now be creating inefficiencies because product mix has shifted.*

The retirement of a key Engineering manager left a void in the department and the team has become unfocused and disengaged.

Your business team is an organic entity. Regular and consistent practice is the key to maintaining and strengthening your effectiveness, just as maintaining a good diet and exercising are critical to your personal health. Practices in this book that strike you now as low-impact, may become the most critical ones in the future. And today's home-runs may become insignificant tomorrow. The practice of building teams to produce profits goes on.

Practice is also important because it has a very powerful psychological effect on both individuals and the organization as a whole. How we think largely determines how we act and our actions determine what we will achieve. When you believe something is out of your reach, too hard, too big or otherwise unattainable, it almost certainly will become exactly that. Or, as Richard Bach wrote is his inspiring novel **Illusions**, "Argue for your limitations, and sure enough they're yours."[1]

The process is circular. When your efforts to accomplish something repeatedly fail, it reinforces the belief it's too difficult, it can't be done, or is out of your reach. Not everyone is derailed by this, but it's not difficult to imagine the interaction between what we believe and the results we get. Thoughts become actions, actions become results, and results influence thought.

The beauty is you can turn it to work in your favor, through the practices in this book. Becoming a highly effective team is not an insignificant task. And it can seem a little daunting, especially if your business team is struggling. For the most part the practices are relatively small undertakings individually. Even using one of them will enable you to affect changes with visible results. This will strengthen not only your own beliefs in being able to overcome obstacles and reach your goals, but also those of the people around you.

The more you practice, the better you get. The better you get, the more you believe you can accomplish, and the more you will continue to practice. Creating these self-reinforcing virtuous cycles is the business equivalent of starting the snowball down the hill. The big lesson is that you don't have to solve, or even take on, everything at once. What you need to do is to create *momentum*.

And don't underestimate the impact you and your efforts will have on those around you. When day after day I see my neighbor running past my house on his way for home, sweating and breathing hard, it motivates me to get out of my chair and exercise too. As you model effective teamwork with these common sense practices, it will not go unnoticed. Don't be surprised when some of your colleagues ask you to help them or start to imitate your efforts. Being a good example is a great starting point for building a more profitable business.

Every company relies on a team of people working together to reach its goals. It's not necessary that every player on your team perform at the same level, contribute equally or by equally happy and satisfied. Such a vision may sound romantic or ideal, but it's simply not the way the world works, nor is it necessary to creating a profitable, growing business. Don't get bogged down or frustrated trying to reach everyone, you never will. The more people you do reach though the more the forces will work in your favor to bring more and more people on board.

At the same time, even the best individuals who contribute the most to your business cannot do it alone. Most companies rely heavily on their strongest performers, and you will always have a disparity between your best and worst performers—not everyone will be Michael Jordan or Lionel Messi. Striving to raise everyone's performance a little bit will have a dramatic effect on your results, because the gains add up quickly.

Being part of a great team is infectious. When a group of people learns how to align their efforts toward a common goal and to bring out the best in each other it creates an enormous ripple effect. I've seen the worst business or department become the place everyone wants to work in just a few quick months. As soon as you get a few people energized and aligned you will see it start to draw in others who want to be part of it. So don't worry about how big a task it may seem, or even if the entire company seems disengaged. Just start. The only way to start making the company you want is by doing something about it today. Through everyday practice, focus and follow through, you can turn teamwork into profits and success for all.

Afterword

One of my mentors, Eli Goldratt, used to say that as much as we may talk about it, we really don't want "an easy life." An easy life where we don't have to grow, break our head to find new answers, or overcome many obstacles only sounds appealing when we are struggling. In reality a life where there are few challenges to overcome is not a very rich life and not one that would be very satisfying for most of us.

Building the business you dream about is one of the most exciting and rewarding endeavors in life. Whether you are the owner of modest sized company, CEO of a multi-national corporation, or a middle manager building a career, the only way to be truly successful is to harness the power of your team. While that can be a difficult challenge at times, it is always filled with opportunities to learn, to grow and to succeed in new ways. I believe that this is where one of the real joys in life can be found—in struggling with and overcoming the things that are not easily solved.

When you stretch yourself beyond what you think you can do is when you find real achievement, achievement that is meaningful to the only person who really matters in that arena—yourself. I have found over the past 25+ years of my career that this is where life becomes interesting, worthwhile and energizing. Yes building a great team and keeping it operating at a high level is a difficult task and not one that ever really ends, but it can be one of the most satisfying and energizing of activities. Helping a group of people to work together to achieve great results, doing more than they thought possible and stretching themselves to do more is tremendously fulfilling and a most worthy way to spend your working life.

I hope these practices help in some way to get you over, around or through some of the obstacles that stand in your way. No one can do it for you in the end, and I don't think any of us wants that anyway. But we all need tools, encouragement, and assistance along the way.

I continue to develop and share my learning on the blog www.myviablevision.com/blog. You will also find a place to exchange ideas and learn of new practices and insights for improving performance at the book site, www.teamworkforprofit.com. I hope you will join us and share your stories and your insights with us there.

May your life always be interesting and filled with challenge!

Kevin

Table of Practices- Alignment

Symptoms of Mis-Alignment:

- Organizational Silos are strong
- Department measures look good, but not company performance
- Local improvements don't hit the bottom line
- End of the month "hockey stick" occurs
- Supply and demand mismatches

#	Practice Name	Page	Profit Booster: 🕐 Time Creators	🎯 Doing Right Things	👍 Doing Things Right	➕ Impact Magnifiers
1	Communicate the Goal	31		🎯		➕
2	Share Bottom Line results with Everyone	34		🎯	👍	
3	Replace Local Measures with Global Ones	36		🎯		➕
4	Find the Constraint of Your Business	38		🎯		➕
5	Blue Light Your Business	42	🕐	🎯		
6	Use T, I, OE to Align Decisions to the Goal	46		🎯		➕
7	Routinely Review and Re-align Your Measures	49		🎯	👍	
8	Map What Good Alignment Looks Like	53		🎯		➕
9	Spend Most of Your Time and Energy on Today	57	🕐	🎯		
10	Pareto to Stop Wasting Effort	59	🕐	🎯		
11	Stop the Multi-Tasking	62	🕐			➕
12	Relate Everything Back to the Big Picture	67		🎯		➕
13	Focus on Throughput	70		🎯		➕
14	Use Measures to Provide Fast Feedback on Ideas	73	🕐		👍	

Table of Practices- Engagement

Symptoms of Low Engagement:

- Low employee participation, new idea generation
- Time spent explaining shortcomings not finding solutions
- Blaming
- People keep regular hours

#	Practice Name	Page	Profit Booster: 🕐 Time Creators ◎ Doing Right Things 👍 Doing Things Right ➕ Impact Magnifiers			
15	Picture what Engagement Looks Like	81	🕐		👍	
16	Innovate on Process	83	🕐			➕
17	Use Images to Show 'What Good Looks Like'	86			👍	➕
18	Spark Creative Problem Solving	90	🕐			➕
19	Catch People Doing Something Right	94			👍	➕
20	Share your Ideas Last	97	🕐			➕
21	Provide Opportunities for Growth	99				➕
22	Use Questions	102	🕐	◎		
23	Stop the B-Game	105	🕐			➕
24	Rebuild Trust with Appreciations	108			👍	➕
25	Get Out and Walk Around Everyday	110				➕
26	Follow Through Quickly	112				➕
27	Become the Obstacle Breaker	114		◎		➕
28	Use Financial Incentives Very carefully	116				➕
29	Expect the Best from People	118			👍	➕

End Notes

Chapter 1

[1] Woolf, Henry Bolsey (ed. In chief). **Webster's New Collegiate Dictionary**. G. & C. Merriam Company, Springfield, MA. 1980. Page 1187.

[2] Cox, Allan. "Team Building." Chief Executive.net, Chief Executive Magazine. http://chiefexecutive.net/team-building/ . Posted March 1, 1989. Web. Viewed June 4, 2015.

[3] Gottleib, Hildy. "Why Team Building Doesn't Work & How You CAN Build your Team." Copyright ReSolve Inc. 2005. http://www.help4nonprofits.com/NP_PRSNL-TeamBuilding_Art.htm . Web. Viewed on May 12, 2015.

[4] Cox, Allan. "Team Building." Chief Executive.net, Chief Executive Magazine. http://chiefexecutive.net/team-building/ . Posted March 1, 1989. Web. Viewed June 4, 2015.

Chapter 2

[1] Goldratt, Eliyahu M. **The Goal: A Process of Ongoing Improvement.** The North River Press Publishing Company, Great Barrington, MA. Copyright 1984.

Chapter 4

[1] Biro, Meghan M. "Happy Employees = Hefty Profits." Published by Forbes Magazine. January 19, 2014. http://www.forbes.com/sites/meghanbiro/2014/01/19/happy-employees-hefty-profits/ . Web. Viewed August 1, 2015.

[2] *Wall Street 2: Money Never Sleeps*. Dir. Oliver Stone. Perf. Michael Douglas, Shia Leboeuf, Josh Brolin, Carey Mulligan, Frank Langella. Edward R. Pressman Film Corporation, 20th Century Fox, 2010. Film.

[3] Kofman, Fred. "Doing Your Job May Be Hazardous to Your Career – LinkedIn Speaker Series 2/3." Published on YouTube August 12, 2013 https://www.youtube.com/watch?v=cgJFLR2f4rY . Web. Viewed on April 11, 2015.

Chapter 5

[1] Adkins, Amy. "Majority of U.S. Employees Not Engaged Despite Gains in 2014". Published by Gallup, Inc. 2015. http://www.gallup.com/poll/181289/majority-employees-not-engaged-despite-gains-2014.aspx . Web. Viewed on May 28, 2015.

[2] Pink, Daniel. <u>Drive: The Surprising Truth About What Motivates Us</u>. Riverhead Books New York, NY. April 2011.

[3] Winfrey, Graham. "Top 5 Reasons Employees Quit (Infographic)". Published by Inc. Magazine, July 16, 2014. <u>http://www.inc.com/graham-winfrey/5-reasons-employees-leave-their-jobs.html</u> . Using Data from a June 2014 U.S. survey conducted by BambooHR. Web. Viewed June 2, 2015.

[4] Smith, Jacquelyn. "What Employers Need to Know About the Class of 2012". Published by Forbes, Inc. April 3, 2012. <u>http://www.forbes.com/sites/jacquelynsmith/2012/04/03/what-employers-need-to-know-about-the-class-of-2012/</u> . Web. Viewed on April 20, 2015.

Chapter 6

[1] Bach, Richard. <u>Illusions: The Adventures of a Reluctant Messiah</u>. Dell Publishing, New York, NY. 1977. Page 100.

About the Author

Kevin Fox works with motivated executives seeking to get more out of their businesses, careers, and lives through his consulting practice, Viable Vision- www.myviablevision.com . For the past 25 years he was fortunate to work closely with Eli Goldratt and Robert Fox, the creators of the Theory of Constraints methodology, and with hundreds of talented, innovative business leaders around the world. His unique experience and perspective enables leaders to see their business in fresh, new ways, exposing hidden opportunities for business growth, improvements, and personal satisfaction. His clients have called his work, "Moneyball for Business," because of the fresh, powerful and common-sense insight it has given them on their businesses.

"We are all of us captives of our own success. When something works we adopt the belief that it is 'right' and hold tight to it. Sometimes it helps to re-fresh our perspective in order to see the next path to our growth."

Mr. Fox is a lifelong sports enthusiast, athlete, coach, and a great believer in the lessons to be learned from team sports. He writes regularly on his blogs at www.myviablevision.com/blog and www.teamworkforprofit.com. He earned his B.A. in History from Yale University, and he holds numerous professional certifications. Kevin presents and lectures on these topics at national and international conferences and to business leaders around the world.

He and his wife, Amy, have three boys. This is his first book.